An Executive's Primer on the Strategy of Social Networks

An Executive's Primer on the Strategy of Social Networks

Mason A. Carpenter

An Executive's Primer on the Strategy of Social Networks
Copyright © Business Expert Press, LLC, 2009.
All rights reserved. No part of this publication may be reproduced, stored in a retrieval system, or transmitted in any form or by any means—electronic, mechanical, photocopy, recording, or any other except for brief quotations, not to exceed 400 words, without the prior permission of the publisher.

First published in 2009 by
Business Expert Press, LLC
222 East 46th Street, New York, NY 10017
www.businessexpertpress.com

ISBN-13: 978-1-60649-029-7 (paperback)
ISBN-10: 1-60649-029-X (paperback)

ISBN-13: 978-1-60649-030-3 (e-book)
ISBN-10: 1-60649-030-3 (e-book)

DOI 10.4128/9781606490303

A publication in the Business Expert Press Strategic Management collection

Collection ISSN (print) forthcoming
Collection ISSN (electronic) forthcoming

Cover design by Artistic Group—Monroe, NY
Interior design by Scribe, Inc.

First edition: May 2009

10 9 8 7 6 5 4 3 2 1

Printed in the United States of America.

This book is written for my wife, Lisa, and growing boys, Wesley and Zachary.

Abstract

The purpose of this primer is to provide executives with an overview of social network research as it relates to individual, group, and organizational learning; innovation; and performance. Too often, when social networks are mentioned, managers think of Internet sites such as LinkedIn, Facebook, or MySpace. While social networking Web sites are part of the landscape of social network research, they are the tip of the iceberg in terms of what we know about social networks and the benefits of managing network structure. Chapter 1 identifies the key conceptual underpinnings of social network theory and social network analysis. Chapter 2 relates how social network theory predicts individual promotion and resource acquisition, while chapter 3 helps you understand and develop tactics for making your social network useful. Chapter 4 extends this work to show how the fruits of team collaboration are dependent on social network characteristics. Chapter 5 looks at social networks through a strategic lens, drawing on examples from Procter & Gamble (the connect and develop model), McKinsey (social networks as invisible organizational structure), and Accenture (innovation in a flat world). Finally, Chapter 6 identifies some of the key ethical issues accompanying social network analysis.

Keywords

Social networks, social capital, strategy, organization structure, human capital

Contents

List of Illustrations ix

Introduction 1

Chapter 1: Social Network Essentials 3

Chapter 2: Social Networks and Individual Performance 11

Chapter 3: Creating Useful Social Networks 23

Chapter 4: Social Networks and Collaboration 49

Chapter 5: Social Networks in Action 57

Chapter 6: Ethical Considerations With
          Social Network Analysis 69

Appendix A: Network Terms and Measures 77

Appendix B: A Brief Survey of Your Social Network 81

Appendix C: Attitudes and Behaviors Conducive
          to Building Useful Social Networks 89

Appendix D: Additional Readings and
          Cases on Social Networks 91

Notes 103

References 107

Index 111

Illustrations

Figure 1: An Example of a Social Network Diagram. 7

Figure 2: How Weak Ties Can Be Strong Bridges 18

Figure 3: Managing the Innovation Network 59

Figure 4: Comparing the Vertical
and Horizontal Organizations 62

Figure 5: The Horizontal Organization as a Network 63

Figure 6: Sample Network Survey Participant Disclosure 73

Table 1: Comparing Network Size and Density
Among Different Student Groups. 13

Table 2: Activities Underlying Each Phase
of the Innovation Network 60

Introduction

I wrote this primer to bring together a burgeoning and exciting literature on social networks and social capital in a way that is clear and accessible to the busy executive or student. While my own research over the past 15 years on competitive strategy, top management teams, boards of directors, and new venture creation has involved social networks and social capital,[1] this book brings together a vast set of resources in fields ranging from sociology to organizational behavior.

One of the reasons, I believe, that the social network literature is not more widely read by managers is that so many of them believe that they already know everything there is to know about the subject, including their own personal and professional social networks. At the same time, they also believe that they cannot, or should not, try to manage the social networks of others. After all, it is through the combination of individual hard work and networking that savvy managers get ahead, right? However, it is increasingly clear that social capital provides the "pipes" through which human capital creates value. Surprisingly, moreover, study after study has shown that managers' perceptions of their own networks are highly imprecise.

To prove my point, consider the following question included in the General Social Survey (GSS), a scientific study of Americans based on a national probability sample:[2]

> Some people have friends who know one another. Other people have friends who don't know one another. Would you say that all your friends know one another, most of your friends know one another, only a few of your friends know one another, or none of your friends know one another?
>
> Check one box:
> [ ] All of my friends know one another
> [ ] Most of my friends know one another
> [ ] Only a few of my friends know one another
> [ ] None of my friends know one another

The results of the survey were somewhat shocking. Even after accounting for age, education, income, and other factors, individuals' perceptions of the extent to which friends knew one another were essentially unrelated to the actual extent to which they knew each other. The good news is that you can improve your scores on such surveys, and this book is a good starting point on your path to improvement. More importantly, you will know how to better manage social capital, yours and that of others, to improve individual and group performance.

A second reason for managers' lack of familiarity with research in social networks is that it may be hard for them to see the overarching patterns. Fortunately, there appear to be common bodies of discussion emerging around the subjects of social networks and social capital. My objective is to further distill this work into a single, concise resource that covers both social networks and social capital and helps managers understand the relationship between them. With this common ground in place, I am hopeful that you are motivated to read the great works on which my synthesis is based.[3]

CHAPTER 1

Social Network Essentials

You know the saying, "It's not *what* you know, it's *who* you know"? Who you know comprises your social network, which, in turn, contributes to social capital. Indeed, if asked, most people will say that social networks and social capital are important. However, you might be surprised to learn that many executives, based on their own experience or what they have learned in business school, do little to assess, support, or actively manage social networks in their own organizations.[1] This neglect is based on the misplaced beliefs that social networks and, by extension, social capital (a) are not manageable (since social networks rarely show up or match up with the organization chart); (b) are the same as "networking," which is an individual function; (c) are a time sink for themselves or their employees; (d) open up the organization to the risk that a critical but hyperconnected individual may leave; or (e) are external in the sense that they exist outside the organization or occupy the space of social networking Web sites like LinkedIn or Facebook.

One of the barriers to the active management of social networks stems from the simple but misleading use of the word *informal*, as in "informal networks," when referring to social networks. That is, social networks are comprised of informal groups of individuals. Unfortunately, while social networks are at their best when they are flexible (i.e., they can be formed and reformed around needs and knowledge), this *informal* description leads many managers to think that social networks are anonymous and passive. And where managers might expect a social network to exist in theory, because that is how they would hope or expect the work in their organization is getting done, that same network may not actually exist in practice. Indeed, research has shown that managers often have an inaccurate understanding of the social networks around them.[2]

Instead, I want you to understand that social networks are very personalized and active, but, absent some measurement and attention, network connections can be somewhat random or disjointed, particularly with regard to one's perceptions of the social networks of others. Social networks are the fabric created by social relationships, and your actions can help determine whether this fabric repels good ideas or is porous so it soaks up information like a sponge. So, from this point forward, I encourage you to banish the notion of "informal network" from your thinking and instead think of social networks in the same way you think about and manage other formal organizational structures, systems, and key organizational processes.

In this book I hope to dispel other widely held but dangerously misleading "myths" about social networks and, by extension, social capital.[3] In the chapters that follow, I draw on current research in the social sciences to show how social networks can be assessed and managed. For example, one of the reasons you likely hired those last sales representatives was because they have a great Rolodex—that is, they have a great network and social capital related to the business development needs of your business.

Furthermore, there is evidence that social networks can be the basis for personal and organizational competitive advantage.[4] Assume for a moment that social networks create value. If everyone had similar social networks, then no single individual would appear to have a demonstrable advantage in terms of social capital. Or, advantages might go to those with better abilities at managing an otherwise similar constellation of network ties. However, there is evidence that social networks are becoming sparser over time. For example, Harvard political scientist Robert Putnam documented the gradual decline in Americans' propensity to join voluntary associations and other groups. Putnam described this phenomenon as "bowling alone," based on his observation that individual play was supplanting team play in bowling alleys, even though more Americans are bowling than ever before.[5]

But voluntary associations are different than business settings, right? Moreover, workers in business settings probably know about the importance of social networks and therefore would be likely to include a greater number of colleagues in their business networks. Contrary to such intuition, a team of University of Michigan researchers recently found that, from 1985 to 2004, the percentage of individuals in businesses who identified a coworker as a close confidant in their discussion networks declined from 48% to 30%.[6] Wow! Consequently, in the general population, as well as the general business context, it would appear that social networks are becoming smaller and more diffuse and that social capital is decreasing. As a result, individuals with social capital and the intangible ability to manage it are becoming rarer and hence more valuable. Indeed, my research and experience as an expert in competitive strategy consistently shows that resources that are valuable, rare, and intangible tend to provide the most enduring sources of individual and firm-level competitive advantage.[7]

As the Rolodex example suggests, you are probably already actively managing your organization's social networks. Since social capital is declining, on average, your selective active management of it is a good thing. I simply want you to further extend this active management approach to your own social networks and those who make your organization tick. Networks, within and across teams, form an increasingly critical but often invisible structure that guides and facilitates everyday work. For this reason, social networks exist within the firm (not just on the Web) and also provide a bridge between the firm and its environment (suppliers, customers, competitors). Finally, while tools like LinkedIn or Facebook are becoming commonplace on managers' desktops and PDAs, they are not a substitute for actively managing social networks and social capital (and these involve, but are not limited to, "networking"). Indeed, there is little evidence that somewhat impersonal electronic social networks operate with the same level of facility as that which underlies networks formed initially through human interaction. Thus, social networks are based first and foremost on the structure of relationships among people.

What Are Social Networks and Social Capital?

This is a good time to more formally define social networks and their offspring, social capital. A *social network* is a social structure made of nodes (which are generally individuals or organizations) that are connected together by ties. In other words, it is a set of relationships among people. Your social network is the structure of personal and professional relationships you have with others. *Social capital*, in turn, is the resources—such as ideas, information, money, and trust—that you are able to access through your social network. The most common distinction established when discussing social capital is between bridging and bonding. Political scientist Robert Putnam suggests that bonding social capital is good for "getting by" and bridging is crucial for "getting ahead." He differentiates between bridging and bonding by suggesting that "bonding social capital constitutes a kind of sociological super glue, whereas bridging social capital provides a sociological WD 40."[8] Bridging is the function of being a broker between groups and yields access, resources, innovation, impact, and profit. Bonding is the function of becoming part of "us" and yields affinity, efficiency, trust, support, and community. Just by thinking about the social network distinctions between bridging versus bonding, you increase your power to win resources, achieve impact, and increase profits.

Social network is a generic term. It does not imply socializing or networking. Social network *ties* (relationships) are formed by one or more specific types of interdependency, such as values, visions, ideas, financial exchange, information exchange, working relationships, social support, organizational structure, friendship, kinship, dislike, conflict, or trade. Interdependence, though, can be as simple as having the same alma mater, birthday, astrological sign, adjoining offices, or fondness for a particular activity. Such social networks can be mapped with social network analysis (SNA), one of the tools used to understand a social network. For instance, SNA can generate an actual network map, as shown in the sample social network diagram (Figure 1).

This hypothetical example could have been created based on a survey of network members by asking them simply, How often do you initiate communication with this individual about work-related matters? (You might glance through chapters 3 and 6 in preparation for such an exercise.) This is a network diagram based on a predefined set of people, like those in a business, functional, or geographic unit. In this case, we are using the example of initiating communications, but you could use a variety of questions such as, who do you seek out for resources, answers to questions, problem solving help, and so on.

To get from survey responses to a chart like this requires a couple of steps. First, and using the example of initiating communication, you might use a scale of 1 (infrequent) to 5 (very frequent or daily) and

Janet is a "connector" with 6 direct links to other nodes; Cindi has only 3 connections but holds a powerful position as the sole "boundary spanner" between different groups; Jeff and Judy have the shortest paths to all others. They have an excellent view of what's going on.

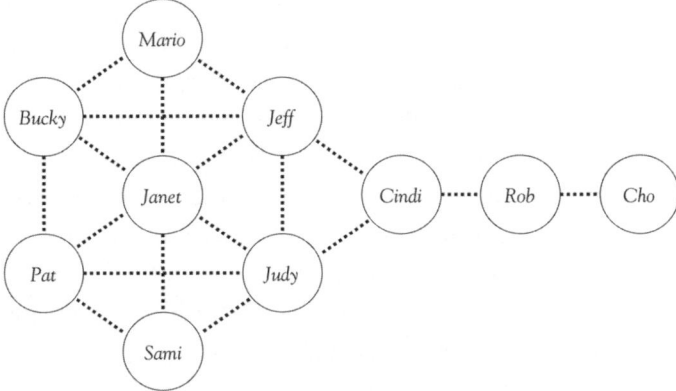

Figure 1. An Example of a Social Network Diagram
Source: Mason A. Carpenter

determine which level of frequency merits a line or link. Second, you would assign arrows to the direction of information flow. Arrows point to those who "initiate frequent conversations"; bidirectional arrows mean that both individuals initiate communication frequently.

Beyond key terms like social networks, social capital, network members, direct and indirect ties, and connectors, many of the other social networks terms I will employ in this book are summarized in appendix A. Referring back to Figure 1, the sample social network diagram, we can see several more distinct social network features. For example, this network has 10 members. There is also one fairly distinct subgroup on the left side of the figure. This subgroup is a form of *clique*, since members are tied to each other within groups but not across them. Without doing the actual math, you can also observe that one individual—Janet—seems more central than the others. Cindi is also a connector, particularly in terms of *betweenness centrality* (centrality with respect to the constituencies on the right and left). This same individual might also be a connector, *critical person*, or *boundary spanner*, because the connection between the right- and left-hand groups would be lost if this individual were to leave.

The Ride of Paul Revere

Before delving further into social network concepts, let's explore the well-known (and lesser known) stories of Paul Revere (and William Dawes). For most American schoolchildren, this story has become a legend. Specifically, Paul Revere rode from Boston one early morning in April 1775 to warn the surrounding communities that the British were on their way. By the time the British had begun their march toward Lexington, on the following day, the colonial resistance was already well organized and in place. As a result, the British were soundly beaten at Concord, giving rise to what history would later record as the American Revolution.

While the result of Paul Revere's ride may be history, let's look a little closer at the actual sequence of events:

> On the night of 17 April 1775, two men rode different routes from outside Boston to Lexington warning communities along the way of the imminent threat from the British army. The message delivered by Paul Revere and William Dawes on their midnight rides was dramatic: the next day would see the British army marching on Lexington to arrest colonial leaders and then on to Concord to seize colonial guns and ammunition. Both Revere and Dawes carried the identical message through just as many towns over just as many miles. Paul Revere's message spread like wildfire in communities such as Charlestown and Medford, but Dawes' message failed to catch fire, with the result that in towns such as Waltham even the local militia leaders weren't aware of the British moves. Why was there a difference in the reception of this identical message? Evidence suggests that Paul Revere was connected to an extensive network of strategic relationships whereas William Dawes' connections were less useful. Paul Revere "knew everybody. . . . When he came upon a town, he would have know exactly whose door to knock on, who the local militia leader was, who the key players in town were" (Gladwell, 2000: 23). Not only did Revere alert whole towns to the looming threat, the leaders in these towns themselves sent riders to alert the surrounding areas. Dawes' message failed to spread through the network whereas Revere's message rapidly diffused.[9]

This simple story of Paul Revere's ride provides a salient example of the power and effectiveness of social networks. It also includes many of the ingredients essential to introducing you to the form and function of social networks. For example, you already know what a social network is—a social network depicts who is connected to whom and is comprised of such features as *network members* (people are network *nodes*), *ties* (the tie between two people, two nodes), and *connectors* (nodes who connect a disproportionate number of people). For example, the network nodes would be all the individuals in our story of Paul Revere and William Dawes. A tie would exist between two individuals if they had some prior personal or professional relationship; indirect ties exist where Revere or Dawes did not have a direct tie to an individual (like *a friend of a friend*, and so on). Finally, the connectors would be those people, such as the local militia leaders, who in turn had links with many other people.

Mapping the Chapters of This Book

Chapter 1 introduced you to the concepts of social networks, social capital, and social networking (and again, networking is an ingredient in, but also distinct from, social networks and social capital). I hope that it began to make the case that, for you, personally and professionally, social networks and social capital are important, strategic, and manageable. Chapter 2 looks at social networks and individuals, with particular attention to what we know about the effects of an individual's social networks on their ability to acquire resources, including the acquisition of information about promotion opportunities. Chapter 3 helps you better understand the attitudes and behaviors that can make your social network useful. Chapter 4 shifts gears a bit to look at the relationship between social networks and collaboration and innovation. Chapter 5 walks you through some examples of how four organizations—Procter & Gamble (P&G), McKinsey, Accenture, and Cisco Systems—have folded social network theory and social capital into how they create value within their organizations and for their clients and customers. Finally, chapter 6 helps highlight some of the potential ethical traps and pitfalls that come into play with the application of social network tools and thinking to your strategy. The appendix contains a summary of social network terms (appendix A), a sample social network survey (appendix B), a brief survey (appendix C) about your attitudes and behaviors concerning social networks, and a compendium of additional readings and cases to further pursue topics around the focal issue of social networks (appendix D).

CHAPTER 2

Social Networks and Individual Performance

When social scientists talk about social networks and individual performance, they are referring to performance in terms of the consequences of network membership and social network characteristics that provide access to other individuals, information, resources, and choices, such as choices regarding new job opportunities. As you know, social capital is the resources—such as ideas, information, money, and trust—that you are able to access through your social network. Therefore, network-based performance is performance due to social capital.

You are probably familiar with the term *six degrees of separation*—though you may be less certain about the term's indirect origins (no, it was not Kevin Bacon). Let's go back for a moment to Stanley Milgram's research on small-world social networks:

> In the 1960s, the psychologist Stanley Milgram conducted an experiment to find an answer to what is known as the small-world problem. The problem is this: how are human beings connected? . . . Milgram's idea was to test this question with a chain letter. He got the names of 160 people who lived in Omaha, Nebraska, and mailed each of them a packet. In the packet was the name and address of a stockbroker who worked in Boston and lived in Sharon, Massachusetts. Each person was instructed to write his or her name on the packet and send it on to a friend or acquaintance, who he or she thought would get the packet closer to the stockbroker. If you lived in Omaha and had a cousin outside of Boston, for example, you might send it to him, on the grounds that—even if your cousin did not himself know the stockbroker—he would be a lot more likely to be able to get to the stockbroker

in two or three or four steps. The idea was that when the packet finally arrived at the stockbroker's house, Milgram could look at the list of all those whose hands it went through to get there and establish how closely connected someone chosen at random from one part of the country was to another person in another part of the country. Milgram found that most of the letters reached the stockbroker in five or six steps.[1]

Take a Simple Test

Before moving on in this chapter, I'd like you to help me conduct a simple test, in the form of a thought experiment. The experiment relates to a survey that I administer to my undergraduate, MBA, and executive MBA students each semester. Among other things, I ask students to record certain facts about their social networks based on the question, *Who do you consult with for questions about your work and career?* The survey has 24 spaces where they can identify contacts using their name or just initials. I then ask them to use a grid to tick off who among these contacts knows the other contacts. I have run variations of this survey every year over the past 12 years, across several hundreds of students, with amazingly consistent results.

The consolidated list of names is analogous to the size of their social network (at least it reflects the size of their social network with respect to work and career resources). Using the information in the grid, students can then calculate the density of their network—density reveals the percentage of network contacts who know other people in the network and can range from 0.0 (no connections among network members) to 1.0 (everyone in the network knows everyone else). So, given this background, what do you think the relative scores (using >, <, = signs) are for each set of students—undergrads (average age is 20), MBAs (average age is 28), and executive MBAs (average age is 40)? Use Table 1 to record your answers.[2]

I ask my students this same set of questions before providing them with the results from their surveys, and the common answer they provide is that the older the student, the greater the expected size of the network and the lower the expected density. And their intuition makes sense,

Table 1. Comparing Network Size and Density Among Different Student Groups

	Undergraduates (18–22)	MBAs (24–32)	Executive MBAs (35–45)
Network Size (0–24)	(>, <, or =)	(>, <, or =)	(>, <, or =)
Network Density (0.0–1.0)	(>, <, or =)	(>, <, or =)	(>, <, or =)

Source: Mason A. Carpenter

right? Early in your career your network may be relatively small, but it should increase in size each year. Similarly, if your network is increasing in size, it stands to reason that fewer people in the network will know each other, such that density should decline over time. Now if you are a manager, then the implications of this intuition are reassuring, since it means that you will likely have a bigger and less dense network than your less-experienced colleagues. Unfortunately, this intuitively "obvious" answer is mostly dead wrong—moreover, it gets further from capturing the true relationship the longer a manager has been in their current role.

For undergrads, the intuition is right on. Their networks are becoming larger and less dense. The rough spot is the MBAs. They form an inflexion point. By that, I mean that younger MBAs are showing social networks that are increasing in size and decreasing in density, while older MBAs are showing social networks that are beginning to contract in size and increase in density. The executive MBAs are actually on the downward slope, meaning that their networks are getting smaller and denser as they get older. Recall that I am talking about averages here, so it is possible for an individual to buck these numbers—and in fact, the purpose of the exercise is to encourage them to do so! My executive MBAs reported an average network size of 13 (plus or minus 5 people) and density of 51% (plus or minus 25%). After my course, where we use the network survey and discuss the implications of the results, students are able to begin making changes to the structure of their network such that their network is more useful.

The Principles of Reciprocity, Exchange, and Similarity

Across all social networks, performance depends three fundamental principles.[3] The first is the *principle of reciprocity*, which simply refers to the degree to which you trade favors with others. With the principle of reciprocity, managers have the ability to get things done by providing services to others in exchange for the services they require. For example, you are more likely to get assistance with a problem from a colleague at work when you have helped them out in the past. Although the quid pro quo may not be immediate, over time managers will receive only in proportion to what they give. Unless the exchanges are roughly equivalent over time, hard feelings or distrust will result. In organizations, few transactions are one-shot deals. Most are ongoing trades of "favors." Therefore, two outcomes are important: success in achieving the objective and success in improving the relationship such that the next exchange will be more productive.

The second principle is the *principle of exchange*. Like the reciprocity principle, it refers to "trading favors," but it is different in this way: The principle of exchange proposes that there may be greater opportunity for trading favors when the actors are different from one another. In fact, according to network theory, "difference" is what makes network ties useful in that such difference increases the likelihood that each party brings a complementary resource to the table. Going back to our example where you sought out assistance from a colleague, you probably needed that assistance because they brought a different skill-set, knowledge, or other resource to bear on the problem. That is, since you were different, the value of exchange was greater.

The third principle is the *principle of similarity*. Psychologists studying human behavior have observed that relationships, and therefore network ties, tend to develop spontaneously between people with common backgrounds, values, and interests. Similarity, the extent to which your network is only comprised of like-minded folks, makes it more likely that you may be dependent on a handful of people with common interests.

Why should you care? Why is it important to understand these three principles? As a manager, you will find your network useful to the extent that you can balance the effects of the three principles. Because of similarity, it is easier to build networks with those with whom you have various things in common, though this similarity makes the network less useful if you need new ideas or other resources not in the current group. A critical mistake is to become overly dependent on one person or on only a few network relationships. Not only can those relationships sour, but the manager's usefulness to others also depends critically on his or her other connections. People most likely to be attractive potential protégés, for example, will also be likely to have alternative contacts and sponsors available to them.

Similarity also means that you have to work harder to build strong *exchange* networks, since their formation is not spontaneous. Most personal networks are highly clustered—that is, your friends are likely to be friends with one another as well. And, if you made those friends by introducing yourself to them, the chances are high that their experiences and perspectives echo your own. Because ideas generated within this type of network circulate among the same people with shared views, a potential wining idea can wither away and die if no one in the group has what it takes to bring that idea to fruition. But what if someone within that cluster knows someone else who belongs to a whole different group? That connection, formed by an information broker, can expose your idea to a new world, filled with fresh opportunities for success. Diversity makes the difference.

Finally, recall the connectors that were discussed in the vignette on Paul Revere in chapter 1. For reciprocity to work, you have to be willing and able to trade or reciprocate favors, and this means that you might need access to other people or resources outside the current network. For example, you may have to build relationships with other individuals such that you can use them to help you contribute to your existing network ties.

What Is a Good Number?

There is little research to tell us exactly how big (or small) or how dense (or sparse) the ideal network should be, although there are some facts to consider. Some studies have suggested an upper limit of 150 network ties, but that is a pretty big number if you also characterize those ties as very close. When my students analyze their social networks, I ask them to categorize their contacts based on whether their relationship is very close (i.e., they see them frequently) or close to distant (i.e., they see them less than once a month). It is perhaps more reasonable if a few are very close and the rest are spread out in the close to distant categories. If you have a network of 15 to 20 people whose names come to mind quickly, that is probably a useful size, particularly if your network density is around the median of .50. Remember, you just set up a network where you were sort of the center point, and each member of your network, even if they are peripheral to yours, is the center of his or her own network.

A "good" number for density is between .40 and .60—that is, some people know each other and some do not. The advantage of having people in your network who know each other is that they are likely to communicate more frequently and provide a set of shared relationships that you can use to move information, ideas, and other resources forward. Also, if none of your network members knows each other and someone leaves your network for some reason, then you will no longer have access to the great stuff that tie provided you.

Finally, you might want to consider how many individuals in your network are connectors, such as the role Paul Revere played in spreading the news about the British invasion. We can look more recently to Milgram's experiment with the letters from Omaha to Boston to see that, even in that case, 16 of the 24 letters that made it went through the same last person, with most of the balance coming through two other men. If most of the members of your network are the consequence of one or a few people, then you might give some thought to lessening this dependency. Indeed, you also want a number of unique ties, since those relationships provide you access to unique information, resources, ideas, and so on. Due to the network theory principles of reciprocity and exchange, your network is likely to be more responsive when you have helped others in the network (reciprocate favors), and such reciprocation is most likely when you have access to unique resources (the exchange principle).

Explaining the Results

So, going back to my experiment with my students, what is going on here? Why, on average, would your social network grow smaller and denser over time? Part of the answer lies in the tendency of human nature to seek efficiencies. Over time, you figure out how to get work done and who in your network helps you most effectively. Moreover, this sorting out process tends to reduce the size of your network, at least in terms of the individuals who you regularly interact with. Network size decreases alone will lead to greater density, by definition. However, another principle, the similarity principle, also leads us to be more likely to interact with others who are more like us, and these folks tend to be connected. Density increases as a result of network size decreases, compounded by the consequences of the similarity principle.

Dense, small networks are not a bad thing. However, they do serve a narrow set of purposes. Where team effort is necessary and timing is tight, small densely connected teams tend to perform the best. Most of the examples supporting this type of network structure come from sports or the military. For example, it is hard to imagine a soccer or basketball team doing really well if it is comprised of star players who have never worked together before. Similarly, an elite team of commandos would find it hard to be effective if they had no prior working relationships (and the trust that accompanies such relationships).

However, absent other network relationships, the individuals in the sports and military examples would have dense networks that create potential problems as well. Since the only contacts these individuals have are with those in the dense network, new information will not come easily, or it may be discounted out of hand. Such discounting occurs because dense network members view information coming from external sources as being less credible or relevant, simply because it does not originate from a network member.

Another aspect of human behavior makes such dense networks problematic as well. Early social psychology research has shown that, over time, team members tend to communicate less with each other, instead of more.[4] More recent research suggests that managers who have small, dense networks may perform great in a narrow set of operational tasks (that is, their network is operationally very efficient) but are challenged when they need to develop new ideas or provide a strategic perspective.[5] Let's look at some of the principles underlying network effectiveness, in terms of the principles of reciprocity, exchange, and similarity, and then explore two areas where managers encounter social network effects—looking for a job and the networked organization.

Social Networks and Careers

Our knowledge about the relationship between social network characteristics and finding a job is owed to Stanford sociologist Mark Granovetter. In a groundbreaking study, Granovetter found that job seekers are more likely to find a job through weak ties than through strong ties.[6] He demonstrated that while job hunters use social connections to find work, they don't use close friends. Rather, survey respondents said they found jobs through acquaintances: old college friends, former colleagues, people they saw only occasionally or just happened to run into at the right moment. New information, about jobs or anything else, rarely comes from your close friends, because they tend to know the same things and people you do.

Strong ties, as you might expect, exist among individuals who know each other well and engage in relatively frequent, ongoing resource exchanges. *Weak ties*, in contrast, exist among individuals who know each other, at least by reputation, but who do not engage in a regular exchange of resources. In fact, Granovetter showed that those who relied on weak ties to get a managerial job fared better in the market in terms of higher

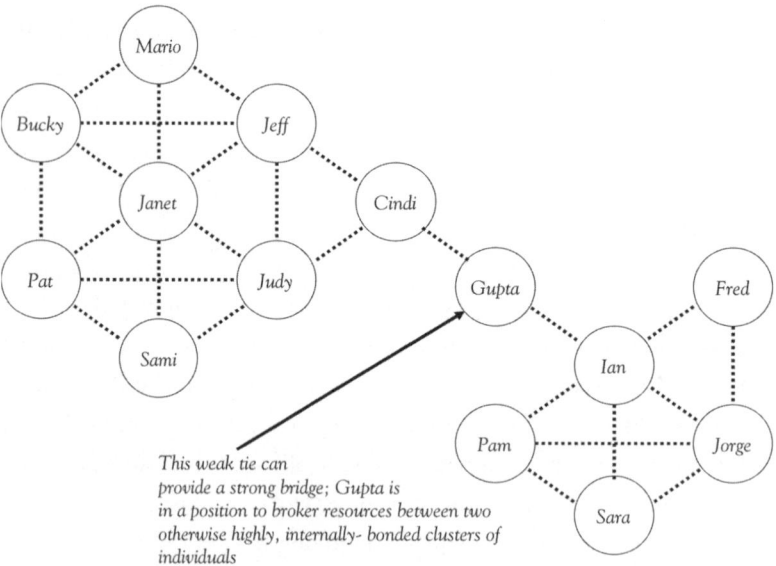

Figure 2. How Weak Ties Can Be Strong Bridges
Source: Mason A. Carpenter

pay, higher occupational status, greater job satisfaction, and longer job tenure.[7] Technical jobs, in contrast, were most often obtained through strong ties (i.e., close contacts). While much in the world has changed since Granovetter's 1974 research, subsequent studies continue to affirm his basic findings on the consequences of social network structure.[8] Not surprisingly, for weak ties to be effective though, there must be some basis for affinity between the indirectly connected individuals, but this affinity can simply be having the same birth month or high school or college alma mater. Such characteristics provide a vehicle for the similarity principle to manifest itself in the form of a basis for mutual goodwill.

The value of weak ties is highly counterintuitive; we tend to think of relationships being more valuable when we have strong ties to others. However, if you think about it, the value of a weak tie lies in the fact that it is typically a *bridging tie*—that is, a tie that provides nonredundant information and resources. In many ways these weak ties operate as key connectors (and sometimes as super connectors). As shown in Figure 2, in the case of a job search, the weak tie serves as a strong bridge. In this example, Gupta also seems to play the role of a connector, since he is the bridge between two otherwise unconnected networks. The figure also represents another deceptively simple insight provided by network research: Individuals who connect groups that are tightly interlinked within but socially isolated across are in a position to profit by the connections that they make.[9] Moreover, it has been shown to be profitable to bridge such "structural holes" in the form of promotion and salary, as well as returns to human capital. For example, in a study of over 190 senior executives, I found that they were paid much more when they occupied a social network position that let them leverage their work experience and education the most. Indeed, executives in network-favorable positions earned as much as 18% more than their otherwise comparably experienced colleagues.[10]

It would, however, be wrong to conclude that the optimal social networking strategy is to build a network of weak ties. Weak ties are very effective for accessing information, but they are less beneficial when you need someone to expend energy or otherwise need substantial help from the other party. This, again, points to the logic that you need to have a network that has a healthy combination of weak and strong ties.

The Networked Organization

This final topic provides a bridge to my later chapters, because it is a topic that has implications for individual performance as well as the performance of the firm. Specifically, as organizations remove layers of hierarchy, and become flatter, they inevitably take on what might be called social network characteristics. The most obvious example of such organizational structure is the case of a matrix, where an employee has two or more bosses, and each of those bosses may have several as well.

The "networked" organization has implications for individual performance for at least two reasons. First, whether the change is explicit or implicit, a move to a network structure also tends to mean a move away from a command-and-control decision-making process to one that is more "democratic." However, unlike the democratic voting process where one person gets one vote, democracy in a network structure tends to be dominated by individuals with the best negotiating skills and positions from which to negotiate. Simply understanding the principles of reciprocity, similarity, and exchange will put you in a better negotiating position since you understand the underlying determinants of social capital and network effectiveness. Moreover, your position is further enhanced when, due to your actual situation, you have something valuable to trade. The manager in a network structure without such natural resource endowments has to more actively create opportunities to trade, and this is both difficult and time-consuming.

Second, the successful individuals in organizations that have strong, embedded network structures tend to take their understanding of the network for granted, such that new hires are left to sink or swim. On the one hand, the elimination of hierarchy is very positive and empowering. On the other hand, absent some form of guide or roadmap, these powerful potential benefits can become frustrated simply because new employees or managers have to find the network in a trial-and-error fashion to get their work accomplished. While it is true that in most firms the organization chart is not a chart of how work is actually done, it takes a certain level of experience and another set of skills—negotiation and social networking skills new to many managers—to divine and navigate an invisible structure when no formal organizational structure exists. While some of the best companies in the world, ranging from Cisco Systems to Pixar to McKinsey, are embracing an organizational form much like a social network, they are effective because they are equipping individuals with an understanding of social networks and the managerial tools to navigate in them effectively.

CHAPTER 3

Creating Useful Social Networks

Worry not that no one knows you, seek to be worth knowing.

—*Confucius*

Your social network is "useful" to the extent that it helps you get your work done more effectively and efficiently. Is your social network useful, and what can you do to create a useful social network?

In this chapter you will explore your attitudes and behaviors toward social networks and social networking. It is important to recognize that, while there is research on the relative value of doing "network" and other work, you will want to achieve a balance between working on your portfolio of social ties and engaging in other forms of work. That is, you need to be both "working" and networking. Whether your network should be dense or varied, or both, will also depend on the nature of the work you need to get done. For example, the transfer of tacit knowledge requires dense networks, while the accumulation of new information requires varied networks. One of the key factors that determines how much value you derive from your social network, and your ability to build a network that is rich and varied, is your ability to do your work very well. In fact, this is one of the bases for my selection of the chapter's opening quote from Confucius. That is, exceptional skills that lead to exceptional accomplishments are great currency to use in networking. Moreover, there are certainly advantages to being an efficient networker as well; and network assessment and development are learned skills, like many others. And yes, there is a plethora of books on social networking, some of which are mentioned in appendix D. For example, you might thumb through Gitomer's (2006) *Little Black Book of Connections: 6.5 Assets for Networking Your Way to Rich Relationships*, or Boothman's (2008) *How to Make People Like You in 90 Seconds or Less*.

With this background in mind, let's take a look at a number of areas where you might begin attending to changes in your attitudes toward networking, your network's structure, or both. This begins with the simple survey found in appendix B. Your visceral response to taking the survey, beyond the scores you generate, already tells you whether or not you are comfortable with the notion of networking as a personal and managerial tool. Since this book has shown you why it is essential to understand your social network, you will need to address any negative implications of your attitude in terms of the constraints it puts on the characteristics of your social network. Looking further at your attitude toward social networks, in conjunction with the survey results, let's consider the following areas of exploration: (a) your beliefs, (b) managing your network, (c) activating your network, and (d) initiating network ties.

Your Beliefs, Values, and Behaviors Regarding Social Networks and Networking

Beliefs, values, and behaviors are powerful forces. They can serve as filters for the information you process and can provide somewhat reflexive behaviors in the face of challenges and change. Individuals hold differing beliefs and values about social networks, and it is important for you to understand yours. For example, consider how would you respond to the following questions:

1. Do you think about your network when starting new projects?
2. Do you create and capitalize on networking opportunities?
3. Do you include people in your network who regularly disagree with you?
4. What is the balance between your time spent on working versus networking?
5. Do you consider working and networking to be distinct tasks?
6. Do you often seek out strangers to work on projects with?

I am constantly thinking network, network, network! When initiating projects, effective managers think about goals and tasks broadly, and they consider how to tap current and potential contacts for expertise and resources. Early in assignments or projects, we often have a good bit of latitude to define goals and actions that will yield a high-quality output. High performers think broadly at this stage and frame endeavors in ways that require them to turn to their networks for resources or expertise. While somewhat risky, this mindset allows them to accomplish things of greater substance than they could on their own, solidifies their reputation for excellence (resulting in more opportunities), and helps them develop an understanding of what the people in their network are able to contribute.

In new projects or day-to-day work, for example, you might consider continually checking to see if you are thinking not just about your own expertise and resources (or those of the people who work for you) but also about those you can draw on from your network. Similarly, reflect for just a few moments on "what if" kinds of questions that consider how you can tap your network to extend your own abilities and resources. Finally, consider taking calculated risks by relying on relationships to accomplish something of substance.

I create social networking opportunities. Effective managers capitalize on productive networking opportunities (lunches, meetings, offsites, etc.) rather than letting a dislike of social situations keep them from building relationships. If you are something of an introvert, interacting with others can be tiring (see the concluding section of this chapter about tactics for networking when you are shy). Because they are energized from within, introverts have a tendency to withdraw from social situations, and that can result in missed opportunities. Even the most resilient extroverts find that being bombarded with lots of requests—even friendly ones—is draining. Whether because of personality or work overload, we sometimes decide to forgo network-building opportunities in favor of the solitary time we may need to rejuvenate. This makes sense on occasion but doesn't continually justify actions that keep you from building and maintaining a productive network.

It often is helpful to recall the benefits that have come to you from past interactions and remember that more often than not meeting new people and reconnecting with past colleagues is energizing and fun. If you don't enter interactions in a positive and enthusiastic frame of mind, you may as well go home. Your attitude is contagious, and, fortunately, you have a good deal of control over it. For example, our physical condition affects our enthusiasm. Consider how changes to diet, exercise, alcohol consumption, and sleep might change your attitude at work. Finally, when entering a meeting or conversation, find ways to leave concerns, negativity, and pessimism behind. While there are myriad techniques for accomplishing this, simply focusing on possibilities, visualizing success, and simply saying, "great, great, great" to yourself in positive and outrageous voices always works if you let it.[1]

I seek diverse opinions from my network. Effective managers continually challenge their thinking and decision making by soliciting information from a range of perspectives in their network—even from people who are likely to disagree with their perspective. Studies show that by far the bulk of information we get and take action on comes from the people around us, not from databases or reports. Obviously, who those people are can have a big impact on our learning and decision making. As you learned earlier in this book, because of the similarity principle we are naturally drawn to those who are similar to us on social dimensions, such as age, race, education, and gender, or who share a common history, perspective, or domain of expertise. People who are similar across these dimensions are likely to have similar opinions and perspectives as well.

There are at least four tactics you can employ for cultivating a diverse network. First, avoid dealing too frequently with people similar to you (in terms of expertise or social characteristics) or who are physically proximate or easily accessible. Ensure balance in your network across hierarchical levels, functional lines, physical distance, and structured versus serendipitous interactions—relational dimensions consistently observed in high performers' networks. Second, try to maintain a continuum of people in your network in terms of length of time known. New people are often good at addressing technical questions (particularly as projects or jobs shift). More established people who know you well are good sounding boards and can give advice with an eye to your strengths and weaknesses. Third, continually test your plans and ideas with people in your network to improve the quality of your solutions and the likelihood of their successful implementation. Reach out with a nondefensive posture and exploratory language that allows you to test ideas and get others' input. Try not to present a plan with a bulletproof logic that keeps others from engaging meaningfully (this often happens when we consciously or unconsciously just look for people to validate our own thinking rather than contribute to our ideas). Finally, reach out for input and guidance early in initiatives, when new perspectives, resources, and contacts might dramatically shape a course of action and determine the opportunities that will arise throughout an initiative. Early exploration helps frame a high-impact initiative by uncovering concerns or identifying people who must be on board.

I manage by walking around. Effective managers strike a good balance between getting their work done and developing and maintaining relationships (that is, they get out of their offices and walk around a bit). Neglect your work, and your reputation will be damaged—along with the network of people you can count on for expertise and resources. However, if you neglect your network, then fewer opportunities will come your way in the workplace. If you are too heavily oriented toward accomplishing tasks, you may burn through relationships with a single goal in mind. As a result, people may be unwilling to help you in the future—and all too willing to gossip about your attitude. At the same time, too heavy an emphasis on maintaining harmony in relationships can lead to incomplete or ineffective execution of tasks (when relying on others for help), not confronting counterproductive behaviors quickly, relying on friends as opposed to people with the best expertise, and incorrectly believing others will do good work or commit a high level of effort to you because of your perception of the relationship (which they may not share). High performers know that balance between accomplishing work and building relationships is the key.

Not all jobs provide the same amount of flexibility in nurturing a social network, so you might need to be creative to make this work. At the very least, do not get stuck in unproductive patterns or cycles of behavior. Confronting and taking action on recurring behaviors that make a relationship unproductive is critical to your own effectiveness and well-being. Have the courage to address problems early, but do so in a nonaccusatory way that focuses on objectives and does not simply assign blame. Similarly, if you are too focused on relationships, set task-related goals and track your progress against them. Make sure that your interactions with others are somewhat structured and that you have objectives coming into (and leaving) a meeting. Or, if you are too focused on tasks, take time to celebrate accomplishments and appreciate what others have done. Task-focused people tend to hone in immediately on the next set of obstacles or challenges and, though well-intentioned, alienate themselves from those who want their efforts to be acknowledged. Also, consider the extent to which you are attentive to the needs of others. Again, be creative and flexible in looking for ways to accomplish both your own and other people's objectives.

Networking is work too (but that does not mean it can't be fun). Instead of thinking that building a network takes too much time away from work, effective managers consider their network to be an important part of their work, and they invest in relationships that help improve their performance, career, and the quality of their work experience. Research consistently shows that a well-connected network—not a big one, but one appropriate for current and future tasks—is associated with early advancement, high performance, and career mobility.[2] Effective networks alert people to problems and opportunities, help reveal the big picture, suggest various ways people can position their efforts, help bypass bureaucratic gridlock, drive innovation by exploring possibilities among people from different backgrounds, and provide safety nets when jobs are restructured or help is needed quickly. Networks can also yield less tangible benefits, including validation, personal support, mentoring, and energy. In fact, laboratory-based scientific experiments have even shown that people with vibrant networks are more resistant than others to injections of a common cold virus.

To gain a better perspective, remember that it is one thing to believe networks are important and another to act on this belief. Start by scheduling network building and maintenance as you would other important tasks. Connecting with others doesn't have to be time-consuming; online services such as UpMo.com can help you set up a schedule to do this. Healthy networks can be built over lunch or coffee, or in 30-minute exploratory sessions. It also helps to consider the process to be an investment, with inputs and consequences like those surrounding the time value of money. Weed out some contacts immediately—pay particular attention to how people behave and whether they follow through on their commitments and be careful of those who talk a good game. Use the process to continually identify people in whom you should invest more time. Finally, remember to keep track of resources that start to accumulate and the benefits you derive through your network; tangible results will motivate you to continue systematically investing in the right relationships.

They don't have to be a stranger forever. Effective people focus on the possibilities that might emerge from collaboration and reach out to those they don't know—even if they feel shy or uncomfortable doing so. Many people are hesitant to reach out to others because they are naturally shy or intimidated. Of course, not building relationships has a high cost as well. Unfortunately, while better connected people develop network-building skills, those with fewer ties often similarly "learn" how to avoid interacting with others over time. Building a responsive network is less about charismatic and gregarious behavior than creating mutually beneficial relationships by being curious, sincere, and interested. It is important to find ways to counter shyness or intimidation in social settings and take steps to overcome avoidance.

To build new contacts, consider taking small steps in interacting with people and celebrate your accomplishments. Find a role model and incorporate some of what that person does into your repertoire (e.g., continually reaching out, systematically following up on commitments, starting a conversation well and probing with neutral questions, exhibiting open body language, maintaining a positive and enthusiastic attitude). It is also helpful to determine not to be intimidated by a fear of rejection (often developed in grade school and reinforced into a well-learned avoidance behavior). Minimize rejection by looking for people who are likely to be receptive and see mutual benefit. And on the occasions when you do experience rejection, do not overplay it in your mind. If you find that you have no common ground with someone, simply smile, shake hands, and wish that person well in parting. If you hear that a colleague is not immediately persuaded by your idea, don't chalk it up to your own self-worth. Any number of things might have distracted that person (but do make sure to listen to useful feedback and adjust your presentation when necessary). Finally, don't believe that you should already know how to do certain things and that reaching out to others will make you look incompetent or needy. Having a need is not the same as being needy. A need can often be solved quickly; being needy is an ongoing, draining experience for both parties. Reaching out to people is only a nuisance if we don't know what we want or what we can offer.

Managing and Adjusting Existing Networks

OK, so your network survey shows that you have a good network in place, but as your situation changes, how do you manage and adjust your network so that it remains useful? There are at least six facets of network management that we need to consider here. As a starting point, though, consider how would you respond to the following questions:

1. Are you consistent and authentic in what you say and do?
2. Do you manage the size of your network, making changes as needed?
3. Do you make changes to your network when you change projects or jobs?
4. Do you gather resources other than information from your network?
5. Do you follow up with key network targets systematically?
6. Do you catalog the resources and capabilities of each member of your network?

Personal consistency and authenticity. Effective managers are consistent and authentic in what they say and in the actions they take based on their words—both over time and across groups of people. While we shy away from people who send mixed messages and seem to operate according to hidden agendas, we are naturally drawn to those who are authentic. Clarity of purpose, as well as consistency in word and deed, builds a reputation for integrity and creates trust and high-quality connections. In trusting relations, both parties experience more freedom to be authentic, speak their minds, and take risks with novel ideas. Less time is spent monitoring the other person or trying to discern intentions. To manage this aspect of your social network, you need to be clear about your ideas and objectives, both in your own mind and in communications to others. If your thinking is not clear, you may send different messages at different points, thereby raising questions about your intentions. You should also be careful not to morph too heavily in response to the needs, goals, or personalities of various groups. While you need to adapt to different groups of people, inconsistency in your underlying values and beliefs or shifting stories will lead people to question you. Similarly, do not ignore tough issues.

Disagree when you think things are going in the wrong direction. But when you disagree, disclose your logic for others to probe and critique with an openness that shows you are interested in the best outcome and hold no agenda. Always raise concerns in a way that focuses attention on the issue at hand and not on the value of someone's contribution. Finally, maintain confidences and stop others from talking in negative ways about people who are not present. Those who have integrity stand out and are trusted.

Avoid network overload. The second area of network management is a consequence of being too networked. Effective managers pay attention to the size of their networks to avoid becoming overloaded in ways that are detrimental to themselves and others. We are all consumed with relational demands. Delayering, reengineering, and the pursuit of the boundaryless organization have put increasing pressure on all of us to manage the time demands of relationships. The costs of not doing so are substantial. You can become so overloaded by the demands of others that you do not do your own work well. Your ability to be innovative, creative, and attentive to long-term objectives decreases as you react to what others tell you is urgent. Those in positions of authority or critical roles in a process can also become bottlenecks if they are overwhelmed by relational demands. Beyond performance, relationship overload can be a drain on our psychic well-being, health, and personal happiness. More than one high performer I've worked with in recent years left a job because of this pressure. To quote one of them in this situation, he said, "I am just too networked now to get anything new done. My only choice is to leave this job and start in a new situation from scratch."

Effective managers look to at least three tactics to reduce network overload—these are through structural, relational, and psychological means. Structural means to decrease overload include actions like delegating, job restructuring, and reallocating who owns specific kinds of information or makes certain kinds of decisions. Ask yourself if parts of your job can be restructured to take burdens off you and help others get their work done. Look back through your day timer and e-mail lists and consider whether people come to you for information that could be made available in other formats, such as on a Web site or through other people. Similarly, consider whether you make decisions that could be embedded in a policy and procedure manual or delegated to others. Relational means to decrease overload are focused on our ability to make a commitment to others with a specific awareness of the costs (usually time) and returns of each relationship. This is a situation-specific strategy that focuses on the value of each relationship. Are you careful not to commit to friends or others in ways that might overextend you? Do you look for efficient means of interacting with others? Do you prune unproductive relationships (e.g., people who claim expertise they do not have or do not give as much as they ask for)? Psychic preparedness to decrease overload is focused on whether a person is ready to let go of relationships. Can you say no to events or requests that might not be the best use of your time, or do you worry about missing every opportunity? Are you personally able to let go, or do you find yourself creeping back into decisions and tasks because it feels good to be in the thick of things?

Make changes to fit the job. When projects shift, responsibilities change, or a new role is on the horizon. Effective managers adjust their networks by developing new relationships *and* putting less into relationships that were productive for past purposes. Networks sometimes need to change, but—fortunately and unfortunately—relationships are sticky and conditioned by a number of things that allow biases to creep in and influence our own effectiveness. Over time, many of us begin to lean too heavily on existing relationships in our network and do not do enough to develop new ones even when our jobs demand new things from us. Personal network assessments with executives often reveal a heavy concentration of trusted advisors from the functional area or business line where they started in the organization. This kind of network may not give them the best and most appropriate resources. And it introduces an overly influential voice in decision-making processes that can lead to ill-informed strategies and an inability to implement plans because others disagree with or were not consulted on them.

To make sure that your network fits your situation, ensure that you decrease reliance on people whose expertise might have been relevant in the past but is less so now. This does not mean not talking to trusted advisors and friends but thinking of their input as only part of a larger picture. Also try to stay connected to people who provide input or advice that is still relevant when your position or job responsibilities change.

People with whom you have already developed a productive relationship will be sound sources of ideas and resources as time progresses. Finally, do not rely on people for advice or expertise just because you are comfortable with them. Catalog the kinds of information and expertise you need and make sure that you have a balanced and viable network in each domain (or are developing good contacts in domains that are not your strength).

Multipurpose networks. Effective managers draw on others for more than just information. They include people in their network who help them on fronts such as career development, political support, sense making, personal support, and finding a larger purpose in work. Indeed, high performers tend to draw more than just information and resources from their networks. They rely on others for their own personal development and as a key source of resilience. One simple thought exercise often reveals substantial gaps and concerns in this regard. For example, when you look back at your network for those network ties that are important to you, consider whom, if anyone, you rely on within and outside of your organization for the following purposes:

- *Task completion.* People who provide information or resources that help get work done
- *Strategizing.* People outside your immediate domain who help you figure out future priorities and challenges.
- *Career development.* People who give feedback that is helpful for career development
- *Political support.* People in influential positions who are advocates and provide resources, support, and information
- *Sense making.* People who help make sense of rumors, events, or gossip
- *Personal support.* People who help us cope with and get over troubling situations at work or in our personal lives
- *Purpose.* People who make us feel that what we do at work matters, that our work has meaning

Most of us need people in our lives who can provide all of these functions. What someone's network should look like depends on things like career stage, personality, and the social groups on which one draws.

Patterns here can be very telling. Some people (men, in particular) have extensive task networks but rely on just one or two others for the rest of the functions. Such people are often surprised to learn how seriously their network would be disrupted by the loss of just one contact. Others have very diversified sets of relationships and are precise about whom they turn to for what. They have more robust networks, but they are also quick to acknowledge the time and effort required to maintain a large number of relationships.

Put your network in your calendar. Effective managers systematically follow up with key contacts in targeted ways that help build the acquaintance into a relationship capable of creating mutual value. Without some kind of follow-up, the "paper" connections we establish by exchanging business cards won't become more meaningful connections that can yield mutual benefits. Most of us attempt to manage our relationships by using some combination of an electronic organizer, e-mail folders, and our own memory. This kind of ad hoc approach often results in missed opportunities to grow relationships from mere contacts. A systematic approach (whether using a Rolodex, file system, or computer application like ACT, CardScan, Outlook, UpMo.com, or a custom database) helps us consistently reach out to others over time to help develop a relationship. Opportunities often magically appear on those occasions when your expertise fits a need at the right time.

You know the saying that luck is a consequence of being in the right place at the right time *and* being prepared. There are at least three ways you can be similarly "lucky" as a result of how you manage your network. First, organize relationships in some scheme that is relevant to your work or personal objectives and then make the appropriate investment of time and effort in follow-up (e.g., making a consistent habit of returning phone calls promptly) and relationship maintenance (e.g., forwarding information, contacts, or notes on special occasions such as birthdays). Second, after meeting someone new, write a note or send an e-mail to show that you appreciate his or her time and look forward to future conversations. If you have a short article or tidbit of information that you believe the contact would find interesting or value, then be sure to send it along as well. Set up a follow-up discussion either in the initial meeting or after an appropriate passage of time. It usually takes a number of meetings (four to eight) to cement a productive relationship—be quick to follow up and propose next steps. Third, send information, contacts, or relevant resources to develop a meaningful connection. Following up in ways that help others accomplish their goals shows you are listening and able to help, and, over time, begins to invoke the principle of reciprocity. But make these interactions nondemanding. Keep voice and e-mail messages short, simple, to the point, and easy to respond to. Know which medium to use and when: All relationships have phases when face-to-face contact is important for establishing trust.

Catalog the members of your network. Effective managers organize their contacts in ways that help them remember expertise and resources in their network when new projects or opportunities arise. Effective categorization schemes and searchable systems (paper or electronic) are critical to tapping your network optimally when you are faced with a new opportunity or challenge. The ad hoc approach most of us take is heavily biased toward people who happen to be on our minds at the moment, are physically proximate, or with whom we have recently interacted rather than those who might have the most relevant expertise, resources, or contacts. How often have you struggled with a problem for some time only to remember suddenly that someone you know could really help out? How might these lapses affect your day-to-day performance?

Once you have a system in place, make sure to update it by recalibrating your understanding of people's expertise as you learn more about them or as their skills develop. Often we can fall into a trap of thinking about people's skills on the basis of our last interactions with them and therefore inaccurately believe that their skills have not advanced or become more diversified. Instead of assuming that people have only one kind of expertise, ask questions to understand what is new and important in their lives to uncover "hidden" knowledge and skills. Finally, always remember that knowing someone is not the same as knowing who they know or what they know or are skilled at. How often have you been surprised by the expertise of someone you thought you knew well? Make sure to uncover these nuggets in your network. Start conversations with an open mind in order to discover key contacts or expertise that even people you know very well might have.

Accessing and Feeding Your Network

Once you think you have a good handle on your social network and that it is in good shape in terms of serving your present and future needs, it is time to begin investing in its health and vitality. The following questions help frame the subjects to come:

1. Do you come off as a self-promoter?
2. Do you have a reputation for reliability?
3. Do you maintain a balance between what you get and what you give?
4. Do you seek to engage others in areas where imaginations and passions overlap?
5. Do you consistently tap your extended networks to implement plans?

Network without being branded as a "networker." Effective managers do not come on too strongly in promoting themselves or topics they think are important but instead fully attend to the opinions and perspectives of others. People are much more likely to become productive members of your network, devote their discretionary time to your causes, or make a valuable introduction if they enjoy your company and feel good about themselves during interactions with you. Similarly, your network is likely to become more useful if you avoid focusing too heavily on your own thoughts and opinions. Too frequently, well-intentioned people can get preoccupied thinking about what they want to say next and thus miss opportunities to probe into others' experiences. Don't take yourself or your ideas too seriously; have a sense of humor and embrace humility. A successful person who is also humble and gives accolades to others draws people in.

For example, you might ask people what they think and then build off their ideas. Look for sincere opportunities to recognize or appreciate others' thoughts, endeavors, or aspirations (and at all costs avoid comments or body language that show you are either not listening or being patronizing—arrogance can seep through in ways that will forever taint a relationship). Make sure that during conversations, others feel that their ideas and opinions are important. Such conversations make people want to be around you, *and* you can contribute something to them because you have not been consumed articulating your own interests. Likewise, it is important to be able to sense when a conversation has reached its natural conclusion and look for graceful and energizing ways to end it. Effective tactics include restating something interesting the other person said or something you share; indicating that you enjoyed the conversation; discussing future possibilities and setting a time to connect (if relevant); when saying goodbye, using the person's name and adding a compliment, such as, "It's been great talking with you."

Build your "brand." While you don't want to be branded as a superficial "networker," effective managers do strive to develop a reputation for reliability, and, as a result, others bring them into their projects and recommend them. Based on your own experience, you can probably attest to the fact that high performers don't say things they don't mean and can be counted on to do what they say—what you see or hear is what you get. When others know they can count on you, they are more likely to bring you into their critical projects and recommend you to people in their network. Credibility grows from being reliable and acting on commitments—and this credibility spreads through a network, establishing a reputation that becomes a valuable asset.

You can help build your brand by being very clear early in interactions about both what you do and don't know. This establishes credibility in areas in which you are an expert and avoids scenarios where people begin to rely on you for knowledge you do not have. Then, as conversations close, be clear on what you can be counted on to accomplish and then stick to your commitment. Failure to live up to expectations—both explicit and implicit promises—can kill a budding relationship. Don't be afraid to set realistic expectations. Too often, in an effort to please others, we overstate what we can accomplish and end up disappointing people who are counting on us. Also, be careful who you vouch for or send to other people. If you pass referrals that result in either the recipient or the subject being dissatisfied, you will have damaged your network. Finally, when you underperform, acknowledge it, recover, and compensate generously for your failures. Take the time and effort to salvage a relationship you have invested in—people will forgive you, and your reputation for integrity will grow and yield benefits over time.

Remember the "reciprocity" principle. Effective managers maintain a balance between what they ask for and what they contribute to those in their network. As you learned in the previous chapter, reciprocity is a principle that governs relationships in societies around the globe. We deeply and universally feel an obligation to repay a benefit received from another and often give more than we receive. The initial giving has to be done in a noncalculating way without expectation of immediate benefit. However, when we harness the power of reciprocity, our social capital multiplies like a good investment.

For example, consider going out of your way to give first and make sure that any relationship you care about is mutually rewarding. If a relationship does not help both parties, it will usually not endure. Second, look for ways to offer ideas, information, contacts, resources, and, when appropriate, actual help to people who are known to reciprocate. Don't expect an immediate or tit-for-tat exchange of favors, but do be prepared to prune people from your network if they do not reciprocate over time or are not responsive to you in times of need. At the same time, it is important not to become too manic about your give-get bank. However, without becoming compulsive, keep track of your contributions and withdrawals from relationships and make sure that each party places a similar value on things given and taken. The "notes" section of Microsoft Outlook is a useful place for keeping track of favors granted and received. Relationships sour when one party believes he or she is giving something that the other does not value in the same way.

Connect with your passions. Effective managers seek to engage others in possibilities that capture their imaginations and hearts. Crafting mutually rewarding possibilities in conversations motivates people to commit their discretionary time to your efforts. Research in many contexts shows that people who spark enthusiasm are higher performers—as are the people who are tightly tied to them in the network.[3] Those who create energy and enthusiasm for their ideas have an amazing ability to raise their own game and that of others around them.

There are a number of ways to manage this aspect of your social network, starting with a personal assessment of what you stand for, individually. For example, do you stand for something larger than yourself? People are naturally willing to make an effort for those who are accomplishing things in the pursuit of an objective larger than their job responsibilities or personal ambitions. What drives most people to go beyond the call of duty is a chance to do work that gives them a sense of purpose. This does not have to be saving the world; it can be writing good code or giving clients the right advice (even if it costs in the short term). But it does have to be grounded in a value or belief that does not ebb and flow on the basis of money or politics. Or, do you create engaging possibilities in conversations? Enthusiasm is usually generated not in conversations about current or past problems but in a focus on what could be.

These possibilities, or visions, must be inspiring and worthy of people's time and effort. But they cannot be overwhelming: Conversations about unrealistic projects can leave people wondering how much work they're about to inherit. Avoid being overly critical or judgmental of ideas still in their infancy. Where energizers see realistic possibilities, de-energizers see roadblocks at every turn and have a deadly effect on a group's ability to innovate. Consider questions like, What about this as an option? What if we thought about it this way? Have you ever tried this? Finally, are you engaged, that is, fully present (mentally and physically) in conversations with others? Rather than going through the motions of being engaged—something that is much more transparent than many de-energizers think—high performers physically and mentally demonstrate their interest in the person and the topic of conversation in various ways: leaning in to face the person, maintaining eye contact, and synchronizing their movements with the other person's; not doing or thinking about anything else; asking questions to build an understanding of the other person's position; focusing on the other person's agenda and not their own; and remembering key pieces of information.

Leverage those weak ties. As you can imagine, effective managers tap relationships in their extended network well in order to get their plans implemented effectively and efficiently. Getting things done requires resources, access to decision-making authority, and commitment from others. High performers leverage their relationships—both formal and informal—in targeted ways that help them put their plans into action.

Some tactics for managing this aspect of your network include some assessment of the political landscape as well as considering the appointment of one or more mentors. High performers tend to have an intuitive feel for who the influential people are in their organization's informal structure and work through them to communicate information efficiently, help build support for their plans, and acquire diverse expertise and resources. Consider whether you have a good picture of the informal networks in your organization, and know how to leverage this asset. Many of us think we have an accurate view of networks, but research shows we are often off in knowing the network beyond our inner circle of 10 to 15 people. At the same time, make sure to establish, maintain, and leverage appropriate connections to those in formal hierarchical positions who can provide resources or have decision-making authority.

While an excessive number of such relationships smacks of political posturing (and can take time away from getting work done), the right ones can pay enormous dividends when leveraged in a measured way. A mentor can help with either of the previous tactics, in addition to others. Mentoring relationships, a special kind of connection to someone in a more senior position, can provide support, learning, and resources. Mentors can open doors, make introductions, and identify opportunities for you. Mentors do not have to be in your organization and can also help you bridge other activities and identify future external opportunities.

Taking the Initiative

Effective managers do not wait for an ideal time or topic to initiate a conversation. Instead, they systematically reach out to others in order to explore the potential benefit of collaborating with them. In this section you will look at a number of ways to take the initiative in developing your social network. Let's start with several related questions:

1. Do you wait for an ideal time to initiate conversation or collaboration?
2. Do you pay attention to the body language of yourself and others?
3. Do you set up meetings with clear agendas and information about mutual benefits?
4. When you introduce yourself, do you include information that might suggest common ground?
5. Are you inquisitive and ask many questions of new acquaintances to find commonalities?

Sowing the seeds for social network needs. High performers spend time cultivating relationships even when they do not have an immediate need. By reaching out and considering how others' expertise might be useful in current projects or future collaborative endeavors, high performers continually "seed" relationships. This process extends the scope and range of resources and expertise high performers have at their disposal when deciding how to frame and pursue opportunities.

In the short term, you might consider setting goals to meet people to ensure that you are continually developing your networking skills. For example, commit to reaching out to three new people a week. Put yourself in new networking situations more regularly. Plan to meet five new people at the next networking event. Use both established and new contacts to identify people you would benefit from knowing and whom your contact could help you meet. Take a minute to ask other people, "What people do you know whom I should be in touch with?" Over the long term, in contrast, attend to expanding your network by reaching out to people who fit your objectives and are outside of your current set of contacts. Do not reach out in ways that simply create a large number of surface acquaintances.

Make investments in relationships that extend your abilities by getting to people with relevant and high-quality expertise, resources, political clout, or decision-making authority. Such people might include clients (internal or external), those in similar roles in other organizations, people in upstream or downstream roles in other organizations, people in organizations that might be interested in your ideas, past or present coworkers or bosses, people you went to school with, people in professional or philanthropic groups with you (e.g., church or community groups), neighbors or people you encounter during your leisure time.

Do you judge people by how they look? You are not alone in this regard. Effective managers are conscious of how body language (posture, gestures, eye contact, facial expressions, and use of space), appearance, and speech (confidence, inflection, and enthusiasm) affect initial impressions and the subsequent quality of an interaction. As you know, most of what we communicate is nonverbal. In chapter 6 of *Social Intelligence* (2006), psychologist Daniel Goleman provides three sets of snapshots with the eyes of three individuals—amazingly, just by looking at the expressions in their eyes, you can guess whether they are grateful, alarmed, flirtatious, and so on. A well-known study found that body language accounted for over half and tone of voice roughly one-third of the information communicated to others. Specifically, the bulk of our communication comes across in our appearance and body language, comprising 55%. Tone, speed, and inflection of our voice make up the remaining 38%.[4] This finding is particularly crucial for new relationships. The point is that what people say in conversations is often trivial in comparison with what they communicate through their physical presence and tone. When body language, tone of voice, and words are communicating the same message, you become more credible and persuasive.

This knowledge of body language can benefit you in your management and development of your social network. For example, communicate enthusiasm and interest with an open stance, smile, eye contact, nodding, active listening, and an engaging voice. Demonstrate that you are listening attentively by nodding periodically and raising your eyebrows while maintaining eye contact. Similarly, consider the message that your appearance conveys: Are you professionally dressed from your shoes up? Do your attire and grooming help you convey your professional values and attitude, or are they distracting?

Set clear agendas. Effective people set up meetings with a clear and well-articulated reason for connecting (even if only to explore an idea). That is, the most productive interactions and relationships offer benefits to both parties. In setting up a meeting, make sure to communicate your intent in ways that allow others to see the value of making time for you. This makes the potential benefit of the meeting transparent to the other person, keeps you from hinting or conveying interests in muddled ways, and helps you redirect the conversation as necessary. Also, early in the conversation, be sure to look for ways to help the other person. Perhaps he or she would benefit from your expertise, contacts, or resources. This is not a manipulative tactic; it reflects a mindset of seeking to help others before helping yourself. Of course you will only invest so much without a return. It is important to be clear about and not lose sight of your own objectives (information, an introduction, resources, advice, mentoring, political or personal support). Such clarity helps you make adjustments during the interaction, recognize what you might have to offer that is of commensurate value, or leave a meeting knowing you need to follow up with others.

Beyond these general pointers, be sure to state clearly what you would like from the other person. Don't be afraid to make a request. If you don't articulate your needs in a straightforward manner, you may end up hinting, and the other person may not interpret you correctly. In addition, make sure that your request is appropriate in the context of the relationship. Consider such things as reciprocity, history, closeness, mutual goals, and future potential of the relationship to ensure that you are not asking for too much. Be sure that the other person has benefited or will benefit from the relationship and that you have not been taking without giving back. Finally, try to phrase the request in a way that is confident yet creates room for the other party to say no. Prepare yourself that no might be the answer and have a means of handling this graciously. Leave the interaction in a way that does not damage the relationship or restrict future possibilities.

People want to know you. In introducing themselves, effective managers succinctly and enthusiastically characterize what they do in ways that help others see where interests and objectives overlap. Everyone knows that the first few seconds of a conversation can largely determine people's interest in you and what you have to offer. A poor beginning can take a long time to overcome; a positive one can lead to productive interactions. Given this, it is odd that people do little to think through an opening statement that concisely and engagingly communicates who they are.

For example, to make a good impression, you might consider having a planned and practiced self-introduction that is clear, interesting, and well delivered. Nicholas Boothman, an expert in building relationships, suggests having two introductory scripts: first, an engaging 8- to 10-second script that conveys in the first sentence the one thing you would like people to know about you (i.e., what you do and what inspires you to do it) and in the second sentence provides an example. The objective is to make people want to know more. Don't just say, "I am a teacher." Say, "I work with and learn from some of the best students in the world." Craft a statement you are comfortable with—the intent is not to be self-aggrandizing but to convey interesting information that can help spark a conversation. Second, a follow-on statement that is concise (20 to 25 seconds) conveys something about you that is unique or memorable, describes benefits that you provide (not just a description of a role), and is delivered with a sense of enthusiasm and quiet confidence.[5]

Be inquisitive. Effective managers are eager to connect with others and ask many questions—both professional and personal—to find commonalities. Getting to common ground is the challenge with someone you have just met. We want to connect on practical, work-related matters, but almost all of us also want to connect with others as human beings outside of the roles we play at work. In fact, the relationships that become valuable assets at work for high performers universally develop first on a personal front. People with whom we have a basic personal connection are more willing to commit their discretionary time and effort to us. We also tend to have more productive and creative brainstorming sessions with those we know—and trust—because of non-work-related connections.

There are at least three tactics you can consider in building such common ground. For example, stay curious, avoid making snap judgments, and ask lots of open-ended questions: What brought you here? What kind of work do you do? Where do you hope to take your business or career? What are you most excited about in your job these days? Avoid dead-end yes or no questions; instead, ask questions that call on people to use their imagination (What do you think about . . . ? What do you like about . . . ?). Listen more than you talk, and use the information you gather to identify ways that you can offer something of value, such as a contact or specific information. Being inquisitive does not help much if you do not listen or do not attempt to gauge other behavioral cues. Be observant and use objects or behaviors to start a conversation ("That is a neat handheld—what do you think of it?" "That was an interesting comment you made—do you think the speaker responded well to your point?" "Is that a picture of your family?"). Then listen carefully, with enthusiastic and undivided attention. At the right time, ask appropriate questions that establish a personal connection: "Any interesting vacations planned?" "What keeps you busy in your spare time?" "Have you started any new projects or joined any new groups recently?" "What have you always wanted to do but not had time for?" And be open about your own personal goals, dreams, interests, and passions.

Networking When You Are Shy

Are you shy, an introvert? The final section of this chapter puts together a constellation of five tactics to help the shy manager. If you're a reserved person, unlike extroverts, you aren't energized by contact with others. About 25% of us are introverted types who prefer the company of our own ideas and thoughts and who recharge by being alone.[6] Perhaps another 25% are just too introverted to admit that we are shy! But this behavior is the antithesis of what's needed to develop and manage a social network.

While there are many contexts in which social networks create value, let's explore the shy networker's strategy in the context of finding a job. As you know, based on the work of Granovetter and others, surveys indicate that talking to others to gain referrals is how the majority of executives find new positions. Other methods, such as answering newspaper ads and Internet listings or talking to recruiters, are less effective, resulting in about one-third of all new positions. If you choose to use these more impersonal job-search techniques, you'll no doubt gain an offer eventually, but you'll need to work harder and longer than if you're able to network. A better alternative may be to develop less-threatening networking techniques. You can start by understanding the true meaning and process of networking.

Tactic 1: discard incorrect notions. Many job seekers incorrectly view the networking tactic as a frenzied quest to collect as many names as possible; then ask everyone on their list for jobs. No wonder introverts are afraid to network. This definition would exhaust any sane person. Other job hunters define networking as asking for favors they can't return. "Networking makes me feel like I'm begging for a job," says a former human resources vice president at a New Jersey–based chemicals company. Both definitions are wrong. Networking shouldn't be frenzied, nor is it about "begging" for a job. In fact, networking isn't really about getting a job. It's about using shared interests to develop and maintain mutually beneficial relationships. Then, if you lose your job, these contacts will be there to help. Done right, networking is a lifelong, evolutionary process that you should do frequently, if not daily. It's as natural as eating and sleeping. Whenever you talk with others and seek their opinions to make an informed decision—even if it's just to find a good restaurant, movie, or electrician—you're networking.

Of course, this definition raises red flags for many shy people. But if you understand your personality type and your limitations, you can create a strategy that works for you. For example, some people are more introverted than others, and some introverts are successful in fields that normally attract extroverts. By learning who you are, you'll be more open and approachable.

Tactic 2: develop your listening skills. Introverts are generally quieter individuals who prefer to spend as much time as possible in the company of their own thoughts and ideas, even when among people. They need not be shy and they care an awful lot about people. This caring attitude gives introverts an advantage over more chatty networkers, since they're usually good listeners who absorb and reflect on what they hear. This ability to remember what others say and value is critical to fostering good relationships.

Tactic 3: uncover your passions and connect with them. Many introverts panic and become immobilized by the prospect of calling strangers. But by focusing on an aspect of their industry or field, or on a special career interest they're passionate about, they can overcome this terror. What's your passion? What field, industry, product, service, or cause excites you? What do you enjoy about researching and studying? What current events always capture your attention? What new products or developments fascinate you? When you hook into these interests, you'll talk with conviction and insight, which can reduce your networking jitters. For example, pick something that means a lot to you and approach people on that basis. This gives you a focus and genuine reason for speaking to people.

Tactic 4: volunteer to help others. Volunteering with professional, community, and other groups is another good way for shy candidates to gain visibility and develop relationships. Whenever possible, accept volunteer jobs that allow you to show off your skills. For example, if you're a financial whiz, become the treasurer of an organization you care about. By serving as an unpaid volunteer, you'll be noticed in new ways without having to change your introverted style and personality. The same is true if you take on paid, temporary roles.

Tactic 5: use good body language. Besides viewing networking differently, introverts can enhance their effectiveness by improving how they come across to others. Again, you don't have to make a sudden personality change. However, by altering negative perceptions about yourself, you'll build greater trust and rapport with others. Begin by learning to maintain good eye contact. Introverts often avoid looking directly at others, which makes them seem remote or disinterested; coworkers often find this behavior maddening, suspicious, and hard to grasp. But if you never look directly at others, changing this habit can be difficult. The first step is deciding to change. Start by looking at a spot just above and between the other person's eyes. This may seem awkward, but it works. The other person doesn't know you're looking there instead of in their eyes, and you won't seem to glare or stare. You may want to change other behaviors, but don't do anything that seems artificial or contrived. You must know who you are and be honest with people; small talk doesn't fit well for introverts.

These five tactics can be acted on in many ways, but you might consider this five-step process. Networking doesn't mean making thousands of contacts. Instead, write provocative letters introducing yourself, then arrange ways to discuss mutually interesting subjects with a few key people. If you view your job search as a personal research project on a compelling subject—your own future—you'll find it easier to collect critical information and ideas.

The following steps can help reserved professionals become more effective networkers:

1. Recognize and deal with the aspects of networking that bother you most. For example, if you're scared of meeting people, begin by practicing with trusted friends. Tell them about your interests, training, and abilities. Or, if you're worried about becoming tongue-tied, role-play your meetings until you feel confident about what to say. When you took the network survey at the end of the book or worked through the effective networking sections above, where did you feel goose bumps? Which aspects made your stomach crawl?
2. Create a structured plan and then stick to it. Set goals and be disciplined about achieving them. While some career counselors recommend making 15 to 20 calls a day, lower this amount if it seems overwhelming.

3. Make calls when your energy is highest. If you know that you're more upbeat after lunch, save phone calls until then and use the morning for administrative tasks.
4. Know what you want to say when calling. Develop a script that includes your key points and use it to make sure you mention important items. Many introverts have difficulty making small talk. By learning about your contacts and their companies, you can direct your conversations and make them more meaningful.
5. Take time out to replenish yourself. Plan your schedule so that you have periods of solitude that allow you to recharge. For instance, don't schedule a full-day of activities if you plan to network at an evening event.

While you don't have to change yourself, you'll need to learn extroverted skills and behaviors to become a more effective job hunter and social networker, more generally. Like an acquired taste, your appreciation for social networking may grow. And when you start receiving the benefits, your appetite for it may even increase. At the very least, networking is a skill that you can develop, and it will be a necessary one for you to get ahead.

CHAPTER 4

Social Networks and Collaboration

Chapters 2 and 3 helped you to understand the role of individuals in social networks. That is, social networks are the structures of relationships among people. I asked you to think about your social network and the social networks (personal and professional) of others. A social network would not exist without its individual components, the individuals of which it is comprised. This chapter shifts gears to look at the social network as the level of analysis—that is, social networks as a critical vehicle for productive collaboration. This shift is important because the key benefit of social networks, social capital, and collaborative outcomes are not owned by anyone in particular; therefore, an understanding of the larger structure (i.e., based on the nodes or individuals in the network) is essential.

It is important to point out that collaboration is the consequence of skills and behaviors, over and above the network structure in which such skills and behaviors are embedded. Firms such as Cisco Systems that are betting their future on network collaboration do not take the cultural attitudes toward collaboration for granted. Indeed, when Cisco embarked on its transition from a command-and-control structure to one of social network-based collaboration, it similarly shifted its executive reward structure from one where bonuses were based on individual performance to a bonus system based on collaborative abilities and outcomes. As CEO John Chambers noted recently:

> The first year that we [changed to a collaborative system] two of my top leaders got zero bonus. You can bet they learned quickly how to collaborate. And, in fact, 20% of our top management team was not able to make the transition to the new model and had to move on. It's not that they weren't successful working on

their own or that they weren't good people; they just couldn't collaborate effectively.[1]

Since social network analysis (SNA) is a fundamental building block in developing an understanding of how social networks are facilitating or impeding collaboration, it helps to start with an introduction to SNA. In this chapter, I want to briefly review the inputs you would want to consider in setting up an SNA run, and then delve into some of the higher value-added settings where you might consider its application.

Conducting Social Network Analysis

There are a number of great resources for conducting SNA in your organization. These resources range from books (see appendix D) and fee-based Web sites (http://www.humax.net for online social capital surveys or http://www.thenetworkroundtable.org for social network analysis) to the increasing number of consultants who offer SNA (sometimes called organizational network analysis, or ONA) as part of their portfolio of services.[2]

In a recent review of managerial myths about social networks, organization researchers Rob Cross, Nitin Nohria, and Andrew Parker outlined six key areas that must be considered prior to conducting an effective SNA exercise: (a) identify the right focal group, (b) ask the right question, (c) design the survey, (d) collect the data, (e) analyze the data, and (f) share the results.[3] Let's look at the ingredients of each of these six areas in turn.

Focal group. SNA is a blunt instrument in that it can be applied to any group. Since network surveys involve time and money for development, data collection and analysis, and participant debriefing, it is wise to conduct SNA in contexts that you consider strategic. The last section in this chapter provides several possible target contexts for you to consider, but in the final analysis the most beneficial contexts will be those most closely related to the implementation of your strategy. A focal group is also helpful from the standpoint that some survey instruments ask participants to look at a list of names and note who they know, how well they know them, and whether they typically initiate contact or simply respond to the contact of that other group member. As a result, SNA can show you how strong relationships are and, using arrows, the degree to which information or other resources flow in one or more directions.

Identify questions. You probably know this, but if you are looking for certain information, then it is best to start with the right questions. For example, are you interested in information flows, problem solving, who has knowledge about particular pieces of the business, or who individuals trust or seek out for career advice?

Survey design. Experience suggests that you are more likely to get individuals to complete a survey when it has senior management sponsorship and it is brief (less than 20 minutes to complete). While relevant to data collection as well, a design that reduces the response rate will undermine the value of the results. Any response rate less than 80% might be considered a failed effort. For example, the purpose of SNA is to identify an otherwise invisible structure, and since each individual is a node of the network, missing responses leave big gaps in your understanding of the structure. To reliably interpret the results, you will also want to be sure that the survey includes background data on the participants, such as location, function, and gender. Sometimes this information is maintained in other sources so that it can be cross-referenced after the network portion is completed. However, background information is a key input if you are to make meaningful sense of the results. Since you are collecting personal information, and indirectly, information about others (via the network ties), then it is a good idea to have worked through a privacy protocol (see chapter 6) and full disclosure of how the information will be used. Lack of trust in the process will serve to reduce the response rate or prompt participants to be less then forthcoming in their description of network ties.

Data collection. Everything you have done to prepare the survey up to this point will be wasted if you cannot get a large number of participants relative to the size of the target group. This means you will want to be sensitive to the place and timing of the survey and provide an adequate window to complete it accurately. Information technology makes this type of survey much easier to administer online and increases response rates and survey completeness.

Data analysis. Data analysis should take two forms, one graphical and the other statistical. Visible network maps are useful from the standpoint that you can quickly understand the overarching pattern of relationships, and each individual can begin to think about how they might change the current structure of their relationships. Statistical analysis is helpful, too, particularly as you start work with much larger networks. Beyond features like network size and density, such analysis will reveal the central and peripheral players, along with the number of linkages between key operations (as well as the disconnects).

Disseminate results. Finally, since an implicit motivation of SNA is to foster positive organizational changes, a process for disseminating the results should be put in place. The best dissemination practices involve two parts: (a) debrief and (b) education. Debrief is simply sharing the results of the survey, while education is the process of educating participants about social networks, social capital, and how these play into the success of the organization. Outside facilitators are often useful in this regard. For example, the Network Roundtable provides SNA participants with a written report that analyzes the structure of their social network in addition to helping them understand the productive and counterproductive attitudes they have about social networks.[4] Appendix C contains a summary of some of these key attitudinal survey items.

Targeted Social Network Analysis

In 2002, organizations researchers Rob Cross, Steve Borgatti, and Andrew Parker published the results of their study of the social networking characteristics of 23 Fortune 500 firms.[5] These researchers were concerned that traditional analysis of organizational structure might miss the true way that critical work was being done in modern firms—that is, they theorized that social networks, and not the structure presented on the organization chart, might be a better indicator of the flow of knowledge, information, and other vital strategic resources in the organization. One goal of their research was to better define scenarios where conducting SNA would likely yield sufficient benefit to justify the investment of time and energy on the part of the organization.

Cross and colleagues found that SNA was particularly valuable as a diagnostic tool for managers attempting to promote collaboration and knowledge sharing in important networks. Specifically, they found SNA uniquely effective in

- promoting effective collaboration within and across strategically important groups;
- supporting critical junctures in networks that cross functional, hierarchical, or geographic boundaries; and
- ensuring integration within groups following strategic restructuring initiatives.

SNA helps managers see the threads that comprise the otherwise invisible organizational fabric. Whether or not a formal SNA is undertaken, it is helpful for managers to use the metaphor of a social network in every context where strategic collaboration is a necessary precondition for competitive advantage. Let's look at a few examples, using the three areas identified by Cross and colleagues as an organizing framework.

Collaboration within groups. Within strategically important groups, SNA can help shore up linkages by identifying possible intervention points. For example, one recent study examined the social network among members of a large business consulting practice. The practice had been assembled to take advantage of a variety of specialized skills so that the firm could provide its clients with a highly integrated solution. Indeed, the consulting firm's partners had identified a rich market opportunity based on the observation that its clients were unable to tie logistical and strategic needs together. SNA within the consulting practice revealed, however, that the specialists in the firm were similarly disconnected. As a result, the partners of the firm were able to intervene in a way that connected the dots among the practice's specialists.[6]

In the case of the consulting practice, Cross and colleagues concluded that

> the underlying problem was that each subgroup had grown to a point of not knowing what the other group knew (and so how to even consider integrating their expertise in projects). As a result, the interventions undertaken focused on helping to develop this awareness and not simply implementing a collaborative technology or group

process intervention that ultimately would not have addressed the underlying need to create an awareness of each other's expertise. Other common factors fragmenting networks include

- hierarchical leadership style;
- physical dispersion and virtual work;
- politics resulting in sub-groups;
- "not invented here" mentality resulting in networks with dense subgroups only weakly connected to other sub-groups; and
- workflow processes or job descriptions that overload specific roles and slow the group.

Each of these issues demands a different set of interventions; however, social network analysis, combined with some interviews, makes these interactions visible, allowing for a diagnosis and an appropriate solution.[7]

Critical junctures. Critical junctures are those places where it is desirable for functions, geographic units, or business units to come together as a way to realize corporate strategy synergies. In looking at this particular context, Cross and colleagues noted that

> Throughout the organizations we worked with in our research we found this kind of cross-boundary view powerful for identifying points where collaborative activity is not occurring due to organizational boundaries and providing a more targeted approach to interventions. It is important to recognize that it is often not the case that you want high collaborative activity among all departments within an organization. People have a finite amount of time to put into developing and maintaining relationships. With network analysis, we can begin to take a portfolio approach to considering the constellation of relationships that is worth investing time and energy to develop and maintain. [It may not be critical, for instance, that] Division 1 be tightly connected to all other divisions to help the organization meet strategic objectives. To provide strategic value to the organization, Division 1 really only needed

to be well connected to Divisions 3, 5, and 6. Thus, rather than engage in a company-wide initiative to improve collaboration, more targeted and ultimately more successful interventions were employed to facilitate collaboration at specific junctures.[8]

As a case in point, consider the Pixar division of Walt Disney Company. Disney has historically run each business such as theme parks, publishing, and animation as separate businesses. However, much of Disney's profitability is dependent on the creative successes of its animation business, and Pixar in particular, which are then spun out into the other businesses. Any disconnects in the set of relationships linking Pixar to its Disney colleagues and external consumer products partners would seriously undermine the financial impact of the Disney corporate strategy.[9] However, this does not mean that Pixar needs to collaborate with every business in the Disney corporate portfolio. SNA could be used to reveal the weak links in the social network that underlies this strategy.

Strategic integration. SNA can be a particularly valuable tool in the context of integration, whether it is integration related to an alliance, acquisition, or the consolidation of otherwise independent business units.

Again, it is important to understand that even simple back-of-the envelope SNA can be effective. Take, for example, the case of Bank of America's recent acquisition of stock brokerage powerhouse Merrill Lynch. While Bank of America looked at Merrill's brokerage business as the "crown jewel" of the company, only one week after the close of the deal did brokerage head Bob McCann announce he was quitting. One of the issues cited for his departure was that his position reported to an "empty box" in the organization chart.[10] While SNA might not have prevented McCann's departure, it would have revealed that a strong network linkage between McCann and the future leadership of Bank of America was missing.

The Bank of America–Merrill Lynch situation provides an example where collaboration is desired between the present and future leadership of merged organizations. In many cases, however, the objective of an acquisition, in addition to retaining the best managers, is to take a promising technology and leverage it across the acquiring firm. For example, when Eli Lilly purchased Sphinx Pharmaceuticals for its new drug development capabilities, it faced resistance from Lilly's core scientists to adopt or experiment with those capabilities. Instead off allowing the two competing development groups to function independently, Lilly forced its scientists to spend time at Sphinx by making previously in-house drug ingredient screening unavailable.[11] It similarly put Sphinx managers on a more level playing field in terms of pay and promotions, thus further reinforcing the positive social network effects. SNA could be used before such a change is initiated and then followed up several months after to ensure that the new corporate strategy is being implemented effectively.

CHAPTER 5

Social Networks in Action

In this chapter we look at four instances of social networks in action. Specifically, you will see how Procter & Gamble (P&G), McKinsey, Accenture, Cisco Systems, and Classmates.com leverage the logic and structure of social networks to further their strategies and competitive advantage.

Managing Social Networks at P&G: The Connect and Develop Model

Consumer product giant Procter & Gamble (P&G) pioneered the idea of *connect and develop*, which refers to developing new products and services through a vast social network spanning parts of P&G and many other external organizations. Like many companies, P&G historically relied on internal capabilities and those of a network of trusted suppliers to invent, develop, and deliver new products and services to the market. It did not actively seek to connect with potential external partners. Similarly, the P&G products, technologies, and know-how it developed were used almost solely for the manufacture and sale of P&G's core products. Beyond this, P&G seldom licensed them to other companies.

However, around 2003, under the visionary leadership of CEO A. G. Lafley, P&G woke up to the fact that, in the areas in which its does business, there are millions of scientists, engineers, and other companies globally. Why not collaborate with them? P&G now embraces open innovation, and it calls this approach "Connect + Develop." It even has a Web site with Connect + Develop as its address (http://www.pgconnectdevelop.com). This open innovation network at P&G works both ways—inbound and outbound—and encompasses everything from trademarks to packaging, marketing models to engineering, and business services to design.

On the inbound side, P&G not only aggressively looks for solutions for its needs, but it also considers any innovation—packaging, design, marketing models, research methods, engineering, technology, and so on—that would improve its products and services. On the outbound side, P&G has a number of assets available for license: trademarks, technologies, engineering solutions, business services, market research methods and models, and more.

As of 2009, P&G's Connect + Develop strategy had already resulted in several thousand active agreements. Types of innovations vary widely, as do the sources and business models. P&G is interested in all types of high-quality, on-strategy business partners, from individual inventors or entrepreneurs to smaller companies and those listed in the Fortune 500—even competitors. Inbound or out, know-how or new products, examples of success are as diverse as P&G's product categories. Perhaps most telling about the intriguing nature of P&G Connect + Develop success stories is the appointment of P&G CEO A. G. Lafley to the board of General Electric in 2007.

Social Networks in the Eyes of McKinsey & Company: The Innovation Network

Strategy consultant McKinsey & Company points to recent academic research that finds differences in individual creativity and intelligence matter far less for organizational innovation than connections and networks. That is, networked employees can realize their innovations and make them catch on more quickly than nonnetworked employees can.[1]

Based on what was found by Cross and colleagues across many large firms, within P&G, in particular, and from on their own experience, McKinsey has observed four important steps in the innovation network process.[2] These four critical steps in designing, implementing, and managing an innovation network are summarized in Figure 3.

The first step, *connect*, involves the identification of key people in the organization with an innovation mind-set. Such individuals are not wed to the status quo and are comfortable with change and uncertainty. It is important to involve individuals with different backgrounds and approaches to innovation. For example, some individuals are great at generating ideas while others may be better at researching and validating them. This group of individuals would then be defined as a network. The

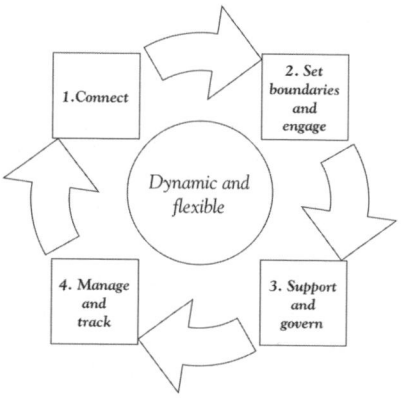

Figure 3. Managing the Innovation Network[3]
Source: Mason A. Carpenter

second step, *set boundaries and engage*, is where the network's goals and objectives are defined. It is important to make it clear how the network's goals and objectives will contribute to the organization's goals and larger strategy, mission, and vision. Time frames and desired target outcomes are stated as well.

In the third step, *support and govern*, the leadership structure for the network is decided on, along with any protocols for meeting, sharing ideas and decision making. With these process guidelines in place, the network members can then make sure that they have identified the resources necessary to conduct their work. This includes gaining sponsorship and buy-in from other parts of the organization, including upper management.

Finally, the fourth step, *manage and track*, covers a spectrum of needs ranging from how network members will be recognized and rewarded for their contributions, the agreement about process tracking criteria, and some guidelines on how new members join or leave the network.

All the basic activities of each step are summarized in Table 2. As mentioned in the *connect* stage of developing an innovation network, you can fine-tune the network's goals by identifying the appropriate mix and balance of employees. Innovation networks, like cross-functional teams, require different skills and attitudes. In McKinsey's experience, they include combinations of several archetypes. Which one are you?

Table 2. Activities Underlying Each Phase of the Innovation Network

Phase	Activities
Connect →	• Find pockets of people with right mind-sets for innovation • Combine people with different approaches to innovation (i.e., idea generators, researchers, experts, producers) • Ensure a mix of people with different levels of seniority and skills as well as performance • Define as one network or include subnetworks devoted to specific tasks, objectives
Set Boundaries and Engage →	• Define role of network in meeting Organization's strategic goals • Establish network goals and objectives, as well as targets for success • Define clear expectations • Establish time frame and time commitment required • Plan how to establish trust among network members and engage them quickly
Support and Govern →	• Define network's sponsorship and leadership • Determine technology support required for network members • Determine role of face-to-face meetings • Define additional support as necessary (e.g., facilitators, administrative help) • Define key knowledge and information inputs—both internal and external to network
Manage and Track →Connect	• Define how members will be recognized for contributions • Establish performance-management criteria based on both individual and group successes • Establish tracking criteria • Define timing for assessment, review, and modification of network, and determine who will have these responsibilities • Decide how new members enter network and current members leave • Plan process to facilitate network and its impact

Source: Mason A. Carpenter

- *Idea generators* prefer to come up with ideas, believe that asking the right questions is more important than having the right answers, and are willing to take risks on high-profile experiments.
- *Researchers* mine data to find patterns, which they use as a source of new ideas. They are the most likely members of the network to seek consumer insights and to regard such insights as a primary input.
- *Experts* value proficiency in a single domain and relish opportunities to get things done.
- *Producers* orchestrate the activities of the network. Others come to them for new ideas or to get things done. They are also the most likely members of the network to be making connections across teams and groups.

Accenture: The Networked Organization as the Structure of the Future

Recent work by global consulting, technology, and outsourcing firm Accenture also emphasizes the central role of social networks, albeit using social networks as a metaphor for explaining the advantages and challenges of managing horizontal organizations.[4] Horizontal organizations are emphasized in the context of Thomas Friedman's *A Flat World*, where people and companies anywhere in the world can compete more equally for jobs and market share.[5]

Horizontal organizations, compared to traditional vertical organizations, exhibit a relatively flat organizational structure. Vertical organizations, in contrast, exhibit the traditional command-and-control pyramid structure. In the extreme case, where the nature of the horizontal organization and its leaders' relationships with employees and customers is turned on its head (as compared to the traditional vertical view), it is the partnership between the firm and its customers where value is created. This contemporary view of the horizontal, individualized company, inspired by business thought leaders Sumantra Ghoshal and Chris Bartlett, is summarized in Figure 4.[6]

The key objective of the horizontal organization is to harness learning, knowledge, and creativity—that is, an organization that is able to direct the flow of human intelligence. In his book *Intelligent Enterprise*,

Figure 4. Comparing the Vertical and Horizontal Organizations
Source: Mason A. Carpenter

written nearly 2 decades ago, James Brian Quinn spoke of the organizational structures most conducive to organizations competing in an economy based on the flow of intelligence around the globe. One such structure he called the "spider's web" organization (see Figure 5), which he describes as operating with little to no formal order-giving hierarchies. The independent nodes of these organizations, Quinn writes, "contain essentially all the accumulated knowledge of the organization and work to a great degree without formal authority interactions most of the time."[7] Importantly, the organization can have as many network nodes as it has employees, suppliers, and customers. There may be a "center" to this organization, but it's one more akin to a "city center": It exists to bring people together, not necessarily to tell them what to do. The center collects and transfers information from and for the nodes.

Accenture's interest in the horizontal organization is not only philosophical, but it is also quite practical. After all, Accenture is a technology consulting firm, and sophisticated information management technologies have long been a solution in search of a strategic business need. Indeed, one of the biggest challenges of managing knowledge and learning in a

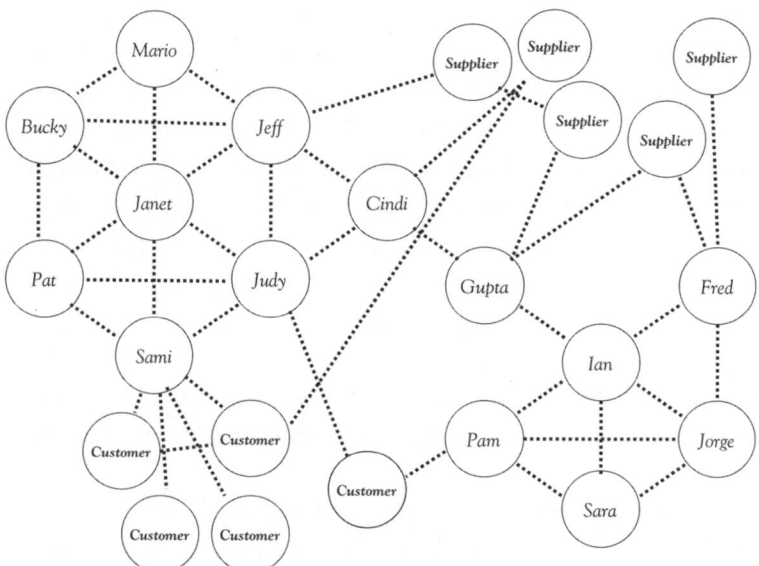

Figure 5. The Horizontal Organization as a Network: The network has as many nodes as it has employees, suppliers, and customers.
Source: Mason A. Carpenter

flat world is answered by sophisticated technological solutions. It is now possible to develop talent anywhere in the world, tap into it anywhere and anytime, and bring that talent together to create value horizontally, owing to advancements in collaboration technologies and applications. Microsoft's Bill Gates, for example, notes that, thanks to the ready availability of natural talent anywhere on the planet and the ability to connect them with collaboration tools, "We're going to tap into the energy and talent of five times as many people as we did before."[8]

Accenture points to two movements that have accelerated the potential to reap collaboration-related benefits from the horizontal organization:

> One is workflow software—standards-based communications protocols and the applications built on them that permit work to flow across functions and locations while executing a single process. When we say that we can send "energy" or knowledge or work from one set of nodes in a horizontal organization to another, it's really the workflow software that's doing it. Workflow software

programs let companies create virtual offices connecting workers in real-time anywhere in the world where there is an Internet connection. A second collaboration-related influence is called "open source" communities: technologists and programmers who come together voluntarily to produce industrial-strength code and applications and make them available for free. Linux and Apache are perhaps the two best-known software products of open source communities; Wikipedia is an example of a product (in this case, an encyclopedia) written by a collaborative community.[9]

Horizontal organizations can be put in place by design, but they also have emergent characteristics. One Accenture consultant observes that

> since an organization is actually comprised of all the individual nodes or persons in the enterprise, every person is either advancing the energy of the organization or impeding it. There are no nodes that only receive energy; all nodes receive it, send it back, or pass it on. A self-forming community may simply not wait for "approval" of an innovation and may execute it anyway. Many organizations aren't quite ready for that on a grand scale, but the day is coming.[10]

Social Networks at Cisco: The Future of Organizing and Management

Management guru Gary Hamel recently made a case as to what fuels long-term business success. He suggested that it was not operational excellence, technology breakthroughs, or new business models, but was instead management innovation—new ways of mobilizing talent, allocating resources, and formulating strategies. Through history, he argues, management innovation has enabled companies to cross new performance thresholds and build enduring advantages. In *The Future of Management*, Hamel makes the case that organizations need management innovation now more than ever.[11] Why? The management paradigm of the last century—centered on control and efficiency—no longer suffices in a world where adaptability and creativity drive business success. To thrive in the future, companies must reinvent management.

While Hamel profiled examples from Google, W. L. Gore, Whole Foods, IBM, Samsung, Best Buy, and other blue-ribbon management innovators, he could just as well have been describing the organization revolution taking place at Cisco Systems under the direction of CEO John Chambers. Chambers calls his new management approach "collaborative management," but it is essentially a horizontal organization structure that capitalizes on the power of social networks, along with aggressive investment and support from advanced Web 2.0 technologies.[12] The basic components of Cisco's network approach are as follows:

- Replacing a vertical structure with a horizontal one. This required Chambers to abandon the top-down management style that characterized his first 10 years as CEO of Cisco.
- Emphasizing teams instead of individuals. Cisco leaders have 22 strategic priorities that are managed by cooperative, collaborative teams referred to as "boards" or "councils." These "are the equivalent of social-networking groups that work together in real time."[13]
- Leveraging leading-edge video and teleconferencing technologies. It has its proprietary Telepresence systems installed in its employees' and customers' offices and even in executives' homes to allow for spontaneous meetings and rapid collaborative decision making. As Chambers says, "With Telepresence, you can literally see a customer's pupils dilate, or watch them cross their arms, and change your discussion based on these important nonverbal cues."[14]

It is important to note that Cisco's core business is creating the ability for networks to function within and across other organizations. Its move to a horizontal organization structure based on social networks represents what Cisco believes to be the natural evolution of competitive advantage in the information technology networking space.

Social Networks as a Business

Social networks can be the basis for a business as well. The largest of these are LinkedIn and Facebook, while Classmates.com is in the top 10. The biggest questions facing incumbents and new entrants to the social networking Internet space are the following: Is profitability achievable? Is profitability sustainable? Let's close this chapter with this excerpt from the Competition section of a public SEC IPO filing for Classmates Media, the owner of Classmates.com.

> The social networking market is highly competitive and is characterized by numerous companies offering varying online services. Our market is rapidly evolving to respond to growing consumer demand for compelling social networking services and functionality. As our market continues to evolve, we believe that demand will be met by a number of large social networking companies. We believe the factors that drive long term success are the ability to build a large and active user base and the ability to monetize that user base through subscriptions or advertising. We believe the principal competitive factors for members are the size of the member base, volume and quality of user generated content and the scope of features. We believe that we compete favorably in each of these areas. However, many of our current competitors, as well as a number of our potential competitors, have more registered users and greater financial, technical, and marketing resources than we do.
>
> Our social networking services compete with a wide variety of social networking Web sites, including broad social networking Web sites such as MySpace and Facebook; a number of specialty Web sites, including LinkedIn, Reunion.com, and Monster.com's Military.com service, that offer similar online social networking services based on school, work, or military communities; and an increasing number of schools, employers, and associations that maintain their own Internet-based alumni information services. We also compete with a wide variety of Web sites that provide users with alternative networks and ways of locating and interacting with acquaintances from various affiliations, including Web portals such as Yahoo!, MSN, and AOL, and online services

designed to locate individuals such as WhitePages and US Search. As Internet search engines continue to improve their technology and their ability to locate individuals, including by finding individuals through their profiles on social networking Web sites, these services will increasingly compete with our services. As a result of the growth of the social networking market, a number of companies are attempting to enter our market, either directly or indirectly, some of which may become significant competitors in the future. In addition, many existing social networking services are broadening their offerings to compete with our services. As we broaden our services and evolve into a service used for meeting new people with similar interests or affiliations, we may compete with the increasing number of social networking Web sites for special niches and areas of interest. For example, our recently launched dating feature competes with a number of online dating services.[15]

Classmates' IPO filing dates from mid-2007, and it is important to note that plans to take the firm public were withdrawn in December 2007 because "under current market conditions an IPO would not be in the best interests of its stockholders."[16] While the stock market was beginning its long march to the fall 2008 financial sector meltdown, it was increasingly apparent to industry experts that Classmates was an also-ran in the social networking market space.[17]

CHAPTER 6

Ethical Considerations With Social Network Analysis

Before delving into the ethical issues, let's revisit what social network analysis is about. Social networking is built on the idea that there is a determinable structure to how people know each other, whether directly or indirectly. Notions such as "six degrees of separation"—that everyone on Earth is separated from everyone else by no more than six intermediate personal relationships—have popularized the idea that people can be (however unknowingly) connected through common associates. As we mentioned at the beginning of this book, social network analysis (SNA) is the mapping and measuring of relationships and flows between people, groups, organizations, computers, Web sites, and other information- and knowledge-processing entities. This can be done with paper and pencil surveys, software programs, and even comparing e-mail and phone logs, but the desired output is essentially the same. Social networks are the invisible organization. That is, they are the actual organization behind the printed organization chart.

Ethical Implications

What harm can there be if a manager uses SNA to uncover the invisible structure in their organization? Three top ethical concerns are (a) violation of privacy, (b) harm to individual standing, and (c) psychological harm.[1] Let's look at each of these three ethical concerns in turn.

Violation of privacy. Managers typically use surveys (sometimes with the aid of consultants) to capture and map the structure of a social network. If each employee has consented to the survey, then the manager is on much more solid ground. Care must be taken, however, that participants are aware of the survey's objectives and applications. Recall that a network diagram reflects a pattern of relationships among people, so that survey participants will actually be reporting, by definition, on what other individuals are doing. For example, if a communication network in your organization is being mapped, you might be asked who you initiate communication with and who initiates it with you. You might also be asked for some indication of communication frequency. So, even if you agreed to complete the survey, the other people that you identify as part of your network may not have.

It is important to note that surveys are not the only basis for mapping social networks. Indeed, think about the network that might be reflected by the contacts on your cell phone or e-mail lists. Given technology today, this data could be readily converted into a social network map showing who corresponded with whom and the length of such correspondence. Moreover, with content coding software, even the content of the e-mails could be coded and analyzed for patterns. This type of social network mapping has more obvious ethical implications because participants of the map may never know that they are actually being mapped!

In both the survey-based and electronic mapping approaches, you might keep the identities of individuals confidential, thereby protecting their privacy. However, it may be possible to *guess* the names of individuals by virtue of their location in the network. First, if certain information can only originate from one part of an organization, it might be pretty obvious to inside observers how such information flowed internally and externally. Similarly, "organizations are typically quite small, so that even a small number of attributes can uniquely identify individuals."[2] Second, demographic information on each person is often available in the human resources database or is common knowledge because everyone knows everyone else. Even if the outcome of such informal information flows are positive, the actual communication may be prohibited internally by organizational rules and procedures. For example, you are likely familiar with the way Post-its were developed at 3M through internal entrepreneurial actions—at the time, however, some of those actions were not an explicit part of 3M's rules and procedures (though, fortunately for 3M, its "bootlegging policy" gave the inventors an opportunity to explore market options for the adhesive that did not stick).[3]

Harm to individual standing. The two remaining ethical issues are somewhat related. As you can imagine from the examples given above, violation of privacy might lead to unforeseen, and possibly unwarranted, disciplinary action. This would harm an individual's standing. For example, if a social network map revealed that one individual or an entire department is the bottleneck for information flowing from one part of the organization to another, action might be taken against that individual or members of the department. It may truly be the case that this person or department is a roadblock to progress, but it may just as likely be the case that managers on one side or the other (in terms of social network) of the apparent bottleneck are not very good at delegating or eliciting information. Similarly, the organization may just be trying to run too much through one particular individual in the network. The information bottleneck that one views as an indication of individual incompetency (i.e., the person who is the bottleneck), may in fact indicate a need for individual training or the addition of staff to move the information more effectively.

The possible harm to individual standing should be noted if 3M had used a social network map to understand the roots of its Post-it home run and had internal policies prohibiting the use of time and money on non-approved projects. If a network survey revealed that 3M's breakthrough was caused by *rogue* employees—that is, employees who were not following the rules about new product development and so on—the individual credited with that innovation might have been reprimanded or fired. This, of course, was not the case in 3M, but you can imagine how organizational policies meant to foster internal efficiencies might prohibit an individual from contravening them, regardless of the benefits of the eventual outcome.

Finally, the purpose of the network analysis may be to identify areas of the firm that just aren't very critical to its mission, vision, and strategy. As social network researchers Steve Borgatti and Jose-Luis Molina note that

> this introduces dangers for the respondents because management may make job or personnel changes (e.g., firing non-central workers) based on the network analysis. In fact, in the case of a consulting engagement, this may be the explicit purpose of the research, at least from the point of view of management.[4]

Obviously, one of the roles of management is to determine the efficient and effective allocation of resources. SNA can be a useful tool in this determination, but the purpose of the analysis should be made clear to participants from the outset.

Psychological harm. This third area can be subtle, but it is very important as well. Psychological harm might arise when information is used in a way that manipulates the behavior of individuals. For example, managers are likely to develop maps of social networks because their managers believe that there might be better ways of planning, organizing, leading, and controlling. As Borgatti and Molina point out, however, SNA in this context is explicitly part of a transformation process in which the group is shown data about itself, such as network diagrams, and asked to react to it. Specifically, "experience suggests that this technique serves as a powerful catalyst for change. It is dangerous, however, because of the powerful emotions it engenders in a group setting and this can put the researcher in the position of practicing therapy without a license."[5]

A Framework for Managing the Ethical Issues of SNA

Now that you understand some of the ethical issues arising from SNA, you are in a better position to anticipate and manage them. Of course, we should refresh your memory on the general ethical decision making guidelines before delving into more SNA-specific ones. In brief, the six steps are as follows:[6]

1. Assess the situation. What are you being asked to do? Is it illegal? Is it unethical? Who might be harmed?
2. Identify the stakeholders and consider the situation from their point of view. For example, consider the point of view of the company's employees, top management, stockholders, customers, suppliers, and community.
3. Consider the alternatives you have available to you and how they affect the stakeholders in terms of consequences, duties, rights and principles, or implications for personal integrity and character.
4. Consider how the action makes you feel about yourself. How would you feel if your actions were reported tomorrow in the *Wall Street*

ETHICAL CONSIDERATIONS WITH SOCIAL NETWORK ANALYSIS 73

Journal (or your daily newspaper)? How would you explain your actions to your mother or to your ten-year-old child?
5. Make a decision. This might involve going to your boss or to a neutral third party (such as an ombudsman or ethics committee). Know your values and your limits. If the company does nothing to rectify the situation, do you want to continue working for the company?
6. Monitor outcomes. Track what actually happens and compare it to what you expected.

Beyond these general guidelines, there are three specific ways that you might manage SNA-related ethical concerns. These are (a) full disclosure, (b) anonymization and opt-out options, and (c) participant training and feedback. Let's look at each of these in turn.

First, you might consider some way of applying the notion of *informed consent* to the participants of an exercise that maps the organization's social networks. This means that each person included in the mapping

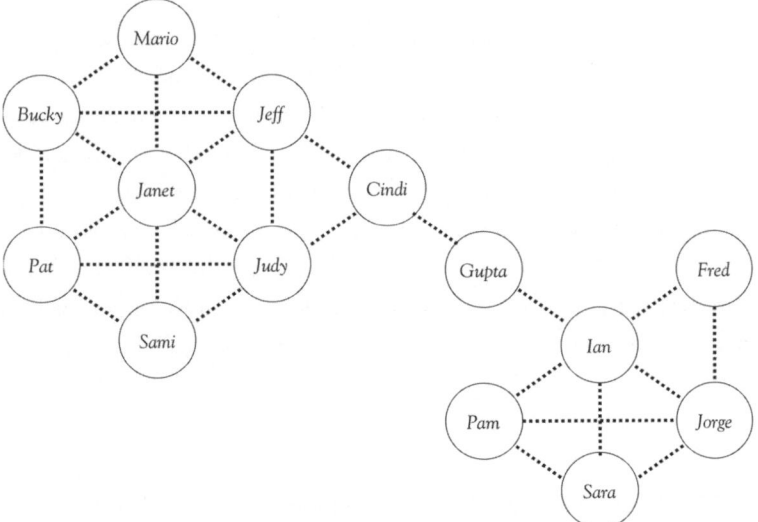

Figure 6. Sample Network Survey Participant Disclosure
Source: Mason A. Carpenter

process would be told the purpose of the exercise, along with what the outcome would look like. Figure 6 provides an example.[7]

Participants would also be an apprised of the possible risks. For example, one SNA informed consent form includes the following paragraph:

> *Risks and costs* Since management will see the results of this study, there is a chance that someone in management could consider your set of communication contacts to be inappropriate for someone in your position, and could think less of you. Please note, however, that the researchers have obtained a signed agreement from management stipulating that the data will be used for improving communication in the company and will not be used in an evaluative way.[8]

Second, managers can consider different ways of making the process anonymous or giving individuals the option to opt out of the mapping process. For example, department-level network information could be presented instead of individual-level information. Where it is impossible to protect the privacy wishes of one individual, then an op-out option is the only way to truly protect their privacy, though this will clearly affect the accuracy of the SNA. If an individual opts out, this should mean that their name appears nowhere on the social network diagram (even if they are identified by another individual as being part of their social network). For example, in the sample map shown in Figure 6, you can see that the map would be very disjointed if Cindi and Gupta opted out of the SNA.

Finally, managers can consider the application of SNA in conjunction with a larger employee development program where participants are taught about social network analysis, and then their results are debriefed with them on a one-to-one basis. Where there are still concerns for privacy, individuals can map their own social networks and then act on them personally. It is important to point out that it is management's responsibility to steward the organization's resources in a way that is consistent with the mission and vision. In that sense, SNA is a valuable tool for understanding how the organization's work actually gets done. However, because it is such a powerful and revealing tool, managers must be thoughtful in its ethical application.

The Ethical Argument in Favor of Managing Social Networks

We close this chapter and book with some discussion of why it might actually be unethical to neglect the organization's social network. It is important to be sensitive to the ethical issues surrounding the management of social networks but that does not mean leaving social network relationships to chance. For example, if you know that your department would be more productive if Person A and Person B were connected, wouldn't you, as a manager, want to make that connection happen? In many firms, individuals are paid based on performance, so this connection might not only increase the department's performance but also their personal incomes as well.

The broader issue is that social networks exist and that the social capital they provide is an important and powerful vehicle for getting work done. That means that the ethical manager should not neglect them. Wayne Baker, author of *Achieving Success through Social Capital*, puts it this way:

> The ethics of social capital [i.e., social network relationships] requires that we all recognize our moral duty to consciously manage relationships. No one can evade this duty—*not* managing relationships *is* managing them. The only choice is how to manage networks of relationships. To be an effective networker, we can't directly pursue the benefits of networks, or focus on what we can get from our networks. In practice, *using* social capital means putting our networks into action and service for others. The great paradox is that by contributing to others, you are helped in return, often far in excess of what anyone would expect or predict.[9]

APPENDIX A

Network Terms and Measures

Attribute
A characteristic of a network member, such as age, education, gender, specialty, discipline, or other background or demographic characteristics.

Centrality
The extent to which a network member is central. Centrality can take several forms: *degree centrality*, often gauged using the relative number of direct ties as a proportion of the total number of network ties; *betweenness centrality*, centrality with respect to the largest constituencies; and *closeness centrality*, network members with the shortest average paths to all the other members.

Clique
A subset of three or more densely interconnected people. A strict definition specifies all possible relationships present; a relaxed definition specifies most relationships present (i.e., a representative sample of relationships).

Connectors
A person in a network that possesses a disproportionate number of ties. When removed, this person's absence causes one or more people to become isolated or breaks the network into two or more disconnected regions. Connectors are sometimes called a *critical person* or *boundary spanner*.

Density
Expressed as a percentage of maximum number possible (for directed relationships, the maximum is calculated as $n^2 - n$); density varies between 0% and 100%.

Direction of relationship
The point toward which something flows or moves, such as advice giving, message sending, or input–output (often indicated by arrowheads in a network diagram). Direction can also be reciprocal (two-way).

Distance
The fewest number of ties between two specified people in a network; also called *path distance* or *geodesic*.

Dyad
A subset of two people connected by a relationship, usually without additional links to other people.

Egocentric network
The set of relationships around an individual, without assessment of each network members' own network structure.

Isolate
A person in a network who is not connected to at least one other person.

Network
A set of relationships among a defined set of people.

Network member
An individual who is part of the network; sometimes called a network *node*.

Outlier
A person connected to only one other person; a peripheral member of a network.

Reachability
The extent to which all people are connected by direct or indirect paths.

Tie
A connection between two people; also called a relationship, link, or bond.

Size of network
The number of actual relationships in a network; often abbreviated as n.

Social capital

The resources—such as ideas, information, money, and trust—that you are able to access through your social network.

Social network
A social structure made of nodes (which are generally individuals or organizations) that that are connected together by ties.

Strength of relationship
The quantity or quality of a relationship, such as frequency of communication, quality of advice, or extent of friendship.

Target network
A desired future network; the object of efforts to change an existing network.

Type of relationship
The content of a connection, such as verbal communication, advice, liking, respect, antagonism, or informal socializing.

APPENDIX B

A Brief Survey of Your Social Network

The pages that follow provide you with a sample of a social network self-assessment survey. I use this survey with budding entrepreneurs to help them think about the social capital inputs into their entrepreneurial aspirations.

As a manager, beyond the topic of entrepreneurship, you might be interested in your (a) communication network, (b) information network, (c) problem-solving network, (d) knowledge network, (e) access network, or (f) career network. A communication network is the structure of an organization as represented in ongoing patterns of interaction, either in general or with respect to a given issue. For example, people on the same office floor may periodically congregate in the break room or by the soda machine and engage in informal communication. For this reason, some descriptions of social networks focus on the pattern of interactions among employees that isn't a direct consequence of the organization chart, job descriptions, and so on.

An information network shows who goes to whom for advice on work-related matters. For example, if you have a question about filling out a form or answering a customer's question, who do you regularly seek out for answers? A problem-solving network indicates who goes to whom to engage in dialogue that helps people solve problems at work. For example, "Whenever this machine breaks down I know I can turn to Pat for help." A knowledge network captures who is aware of whose knowledge and skills, and an access network shows who has access to whose knowledge and expertise. A career network indicates the individuals, past and present, who you consult with for advice on your career objectives and aspirations.

You can assess any of these networks using the following survey, but be sure to substitute the appropriate questions related to that network into the questionnaire. For example, think of the following questions with respect to the following:

- Communication network. Who do you talk with regarding topic X? How much do you typically communicate with each person relative to others in the group?
- Information network. From whom do you frequently acquire information necessary to do your work? From whom do you receive information useful to get your work done? Who do I typically seek work-related information from? Who do I typically give work-related information to?
- Problem-solving network. Who do I typically turn to for help in thinking through a new or challenging problem at work? How effective is this person in helping me to think through new or challenging problems at work?
- Access network. When I need information or advice, who is generally accessible to me within a sufficient amount of time to help me solve my problem?
- Career network. From whom do you seek career advice? Who has helped you progress in your career?

Network Assessment Exercise: Entrepreneur's Version

Introduction

This exercise is based on network instruments designed to help you identify patterns in your approach to developing networks of relationships related to entrepreneurship. Your "network" refers to the set of relationships that help you advance professionally toward your entrepreneurship aspirations, get things done, and, more generally, develop personally and professionally with regard to your entrepreneurial objectives (whether you are doing something entrepreneurial within an existing organization or starting up something from scratch outside of one).

Directions

Follow the instructions for Steps 1 through 5.

Please DO NOT go to Step 5 until you have completed Steps 1 through 4 of this exercise.

Step 1: List Your Network Contacts

In answering the following questions, you may list people from *any* context. It is not necessary to limit yourself to individuals who work for your company. People with whom you have more than one kind of relationship can be listed more than once. In the blanks that follow each question, please list their names or initials. You may list as few or as many as you wish, or leave a question blank if no one comes to mind. If you can remember, try to note the name or initials of who introduced you to each person in this listing.

1. **Discussing important work matters.** If you look back over the last 2 to 3 years, who are the people with whom you have discussed important work matters? This may have been for bouncing ideas for important projects, getting support or cooperation for your initiatives, evaluating opportunities, or any other matters of importance to you.
2. **Discussing new business ideas and new business opportunities.** Who has been most helpful? Consider people who have provided leads, made introductions, offered advice in your decision making, or provided resources.
3. **Advancing your entrepreneurship aspirations.** List those people who have contributed most significantly to your entrepreneurial development and career advancement during the past 2 to 3 years.

Step 2: Consolidate Your List

Consolidate the names listed in Step 1 onto the **Network Grid**. No one person should be listed twice.

Step 3: Describe the Closeness of the Relationship

For each person listed on the network grid, indicate the closeness of your relationship with them by placing an "X" on a continuum from "very close" to "close," and "not very close" to "distant." Very close relationships are those characterized by high degrees of liking, trust, and mutual commitment. Distant relationships are those characterized by not knowing the person very well or by having very little liking, trust, and mutual commitment (i.e., problematic relationships). For an example of how to complete this step, see the **Sample Network Grid**, titled "Pat's Network."

Step 4: Compute the Density of Your Network

Density refers to the extent to which the people in your network know each other. Using the grid on the next page, indicate who knows whom in your network by placing a checkmark in the cells corresponding to each acquainted pair. Leave a cell blank if the pair do not know each other or if you do not know whether they know each other.

Start with Person 1, for example, Lisa in the **Sample Network Grid**. Going across the grid, Lisa knows Jack (2), Jeff (3), and Samantha (8), but no one else in Pat's network. Go on to Person 2, Jack. Jack knows Rick (5), Linda (6), Samantha (8), and David (10). Go on to Person 3, and so on. Once you have finished checkmarking who knows whom, compute the density of *your* network through the following steps:

1. Total number of people in your network
   $N =$ _____
   To follow our example, Pat's $N = 10$
2. Maximum density (i.e., if everyone in your network knew each other). Pat's maximum density is $(10 \times 9) \div 2 = 45$. (*Note*: Mathematically, M can not exceed 1.0.)

$[N \times (N - 1)] \div 2 = M$
   $M =$ _____
3. Total number of check marks on your network grid (i.e., the number of relationships among people in your network).
Pat's $C = 19.$ $C =$ _____

4. Density of your network. Pat's $D = 19 \div 45 = .42$
$C \div M = D$
   $D = $ _____

When you have completed Steps 2, 3, and 4, complete Step 5.

Step 5: Summarize the Network Information

Complete the sections below, make a photocopy, and hand in this page and only this page.

Individual Information (circle applicable)

Gender	Male	Female	
Race/Ethnicity	White	African	Asian
	Hispanic	African American	
	Asian American	Other	

Nationality (by region)   United States and Canada
　　　　　　　　　　　　　　Latin America (Mexico, South, and
　　　　　　　　　　　　　　Central Amer.)
　　　　　　　　　　　　　　Europe
　　　　　　　　　　　　　　Africa and the Middle East
　　　　　　　　　　　　　　Asia
　　　　　　　　　　　　　　Australia and New Zealand

Tenure　　　　　　　　　Years in this industry _____
　　　　　　　　　　　　　　Years with this employer _____
　　　　　　　　　　　　　　Years in present position _____

Network Information

1. Total number of people listed on the Network Grid (from Step 2) _____

2. Total number of individuals who introduced you to these people (from Step 1) _____

3. Number of "very close" relationships listed on the Network Grid (from Step 3) _____

4. Density of your network (D from Step 4) _____ (needs to be less than or equal to 1)

86 AN EXECUTIVE'S PRIMER ON THE STRATEGY OF SOCIAL NETWORKS

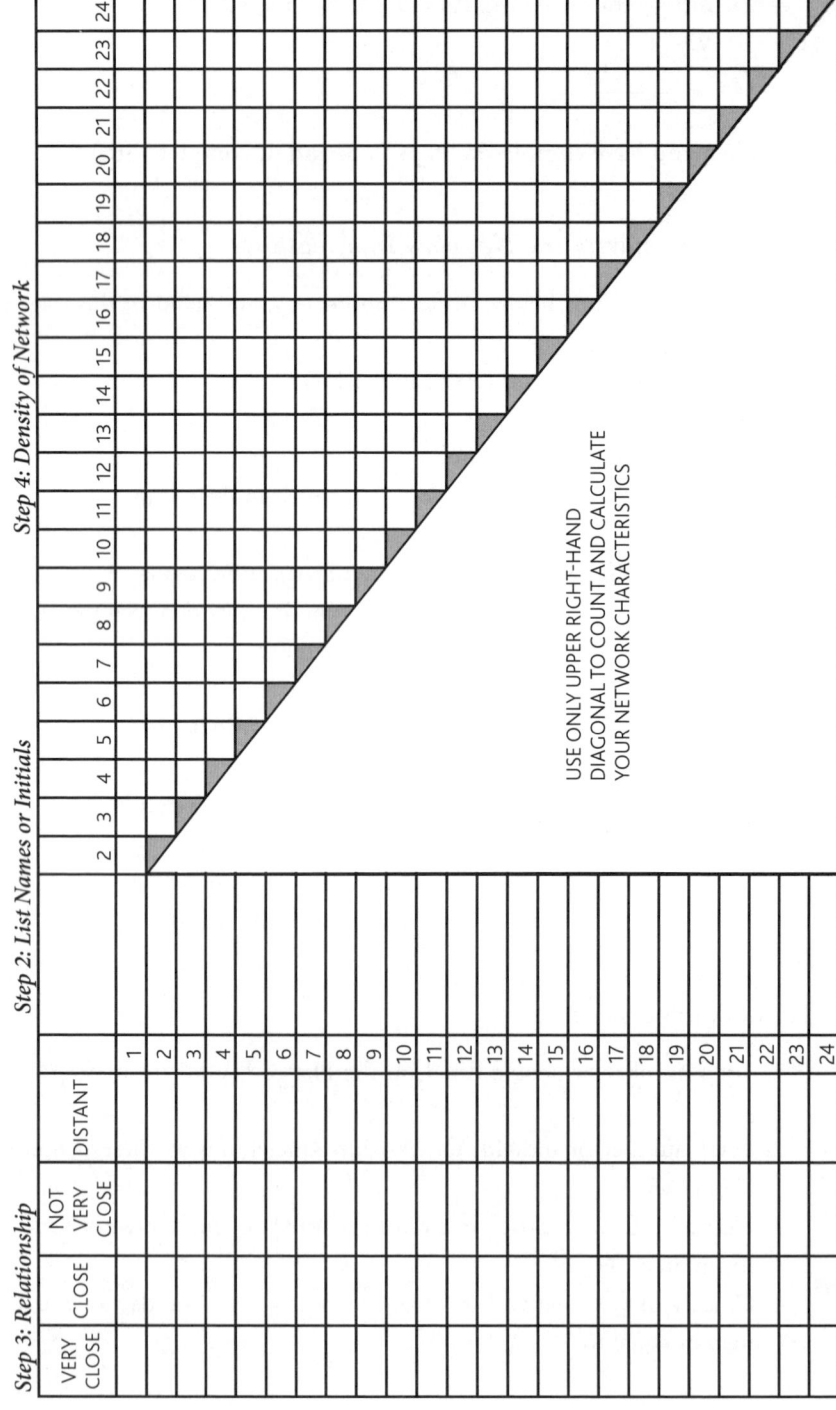

A BRIEF SURVEY OF YOUR SOCIAL NETWORK 87

SAMPLE Network Grid: Pat's Network

Step 2: List Names or Initials — *Step 4: Density of Network*

Step 3: Relationship

	VERY CLOSE	CLOSE	NOT VERY CLOSE	DISTANT			2	3	4	5	6	7	8	9	10	11	12–24
		X			1	LISA	✓	✓		✓	✓		✓				
		X			2	JACK				✓	✓		✓				
		X			3	JEFF				✓	✓	✓					
	X				4	NOAH											
			X		5	RICK							✓	✓			
		X			6	LINDA						✓	✓	✓	✓		
				X	7	JAY							✓	✓	✓		
					8	SAMANTHA									✓		
		X			9	STACY									✓		
			X		10	DAVID											
					11												
					12												
...					...												
					24												

USE ONLY UPPER RIGHT-HAND DIAGONAL TO COUNT AND CALCULATE YOUR NETWORK CHARACTERISTICS

5. Look over your Network Grid and determine the number of people who are

    a) Your senior (higher up in your or another organization)
    _____

    b) Your peer (at your level in your or another organization)
    _____

    c) Your junior (below you in your or another organization)
    _____

    d) From a different functional or product area
    _____

    e) From a different business unit, division, or office in your firm
    _____

    f) From a different firm
    _____

    g) Located in a different region or country
    _____

    h) The same gender as you are
    _____

    i) Members of the same racial or ethnic group as you are
    _____

    j) The same nationality as you are
    _____

APPENDIX C

Attitudes and Behaviors Conducive to Building Useful Social Networks

Evaluate yourself on the following criteria. Areas where you score yourself as weak or you are uncertain of the relevance of social networks are indicative of areas you might consider targeting for development.

1. I think about goals and tasks broadly when initiating projects and consider how to tap current and potential contacts for expertise and resources.
2. I capitalize on productive networking opportunities (lunches, meetings, off-sites, etc.) rather than let a dislike of social situations keep me from building relationships.
3. I continually challenge my thinking and decision making by soliciting information from a range of perspectives in my network—even from people who are likely to disagree with my perspective.
4. At the office, I strike a good balance between getting my work done and developing and maintaining relationships.
5. Instead of thinking that building a network takes too much time away from work, I consider my network to be an important part of my work, and I invest in relationships that help improve my performance, career, and the quality of my work experience.
6. I focus on the possibilities that might emerge from collaboration and reach out to those they don't know—even if I feel shy or uncomfortable doing so.
7. I am consistent in what I say is important and in the actions I take based on my words—both over time and across groups of people.
8. I manage the size of my networks to avoid becoming overloaded in ways that are detrimental to myself and others.

9. When my projects shift, responsibilities change, or I am preparing to step into a new role, I adjust my networks by developing new relationships and putting less into relationships that were productive for past purposes.
10. I draw on others for more than just information. I include people in my network who help me on fronts such as career development, political support, sense making, personal support, and finding a larger purpose in work.
11. I systematically follow up with key contacts in targeted ways that help build the acquaintance into a relationship capable of creating mutual value.
12. I organize my contacts in ways that help me remember expertise and resources in my network when new projects or opportunities arise.
13. I do not come on too strongly in promoting myself or a topic I think is important but instead fully attend to the opinions and perspectives of others.
14. I develop a reputation for reliability, and, as a result, others bring me into their projects and recommend me.
15. I maintain a balance between what I ask for and what I contribute to those in my network.
16. I seek to engage others in possibilities that capture their imaginations and hearts.
17. I tap relationships in my extended network well in order to get my plans implemented effectively and efficiently.
18. I do not wait for an ideal time or topic to initiate a conversation. Instead, I systematically reach out to others in order to explore the potential benefit of collaborating with them.
19. I am conscious of how body language (posture, gestures, eye contact, facial expressions, and use of space), appearance, and speech (confidence, inflection, and enthusiasm) affect initial impressions and the subsequent quality of an interaction.
20. I set up meetings with a clear and well-articulated reason for connecting (even if only to explore an idea).
21. In introducing myself, I succinctly and enthusiastically characterize what I do in ways that help others see where interests and objectives overlap.
22. I am eager to connect with others and ask many questions—both professional and personal—to find commonalities.

APPENDIX D

Additional Readings and Cases on Social Networks

Social Network Analysis Methods

Burt, R. S., & Minor, M. (1983). *Applied network analysis: A methodological introduction.* Newbury Park, CA: Sage.

Freeman, L. C., White, D. R., & Romney, A. K. (1989). *Research methods in social network analysis.* Fairfax, VA: George Mason University Press.

Monge, P. R., & Contractor, N. S. (in press). Emergence of communication networks. In L. Putnam & F. Jablin (Eds.), *New handbook of organizational communication.* Newbury Park, CA: Sage.

Scott, J. (2000). *Social setwork analysis: A handbook* (2nd ed.). Newbury Park, CA: Sage.

Wasserman, S., & Faust, K. (1994). *Social network analysis.* Cambridge: Cambridge University Press.

Wellman, B., & Berkowitz, S. D. (1988). *Social structures: A network approach.* Cambridge: Cambridge University Press.

Business Press Publications

Baker, W. E. (1994). *Networking smart.* New York: McGraw-Hill.

Baker, W. E. (2000). *Achieving success through social capital.* New York: Jossey-Bass.

Boothman, N. (2008). *How to make people like you in 90 seconds or less.* New York: Workman.

Burt, R. S. (1992). *Structural holes.* Boston: Harvard University Press.

Burt, R. (2005). *Brokerage and closure: An introduction to social capital.* Oxford, England: Oxford University Press.

Burt, R. (2009). *Neighbor networks: Competitive advantage local and personal.* Oxford, England: Oxford University Press.

Cross, R., & Parker, A. (2004). *The power of social networks.* Boston: HBS Press.

Gitomer, J. (2006). *Little black book of connections: 6.5 assets for networking your way to rich relationships.* Austin, TX: Bard Press.

Gladwell, M. (2000). *The tipping point: How little things can make a big difference.* New York: Little Brown.

Goleman, D. (2006). *Social intelligence.* New York: Bantam.

Granovetter, M. (1974). *Getting a job: A study of contacts and careers.* Chicago: University of Chicago Press.

Granovetter, M. (1995). *Getting a job: A study of contacts and careers* (2nd ed.). Chicago: University of Chicago Press.

Lin, N. (2001). *Social capital: A theory of social structure and action.* Cambridge, England: Cambridge University Press.

Pfeffer, J. (1992). *Managing with power: Politics and influence in organizations. Resources, allies, and the golden rule.* Boston: Harvard Business School Press.

Other Business Press Readings (Journal Articles and Books)

Bartlett, C. A., & Ghoshal, S. (2003). What is a global manager? *Harvard Business Review, 81*(8), 101–109.

Borgatti, S. P., & Foster, P. (2003). The network paradigm in organizational research: A review and typology. *Journal of Management, 29,* 991–1013.

Burt, R. S., & Ronchi, D. (2007). Teaching executives to see social capital: Results from a field experiment. *Social Science Research, 36,* 1156–1183.

Casciaro, T., & Sousa Lobo, M. (2005). Competent jerks, lovable fools, and the formation of social networks. *Harvard Business Review, 83*(6), 92–102.

Coleman, J. S. (1988). Social capital in the creation of human capital. *American Journal of Sociology, 94,* S95–S120.

Cross, R., Borgatti, S., & Parker, A. (2002). Making invisible work visible. *California Management Review, 44*(2), 25–46.

Cross, R., Laseter, T., Parker, A., & Velasquez, G. (2006). Using social network analysis to improve communities of practice. *California Management Review, 49*(1), 32–60.

Cross, R., Liedtka, J., & Weiss, L. (2005). A practical guide to social networks. *Harvard Business Review, 83*(3), 124–137.

Cross, R., Nohria, N., & Parker, A. (2002). Six myths about informal networks—and how to overcome them. *MIT Sloan Management Review, 43*(3), 67–75.

Ibarra, H., & Hunter, M. (2007). How leaders create and use networks. *Harvard Business Review, 85*(1), 40–50.

Kilduff, M., & Tsai, W. (2004). *Social networks and organizations.* London, England: Sage.

Kotter, J. P. (1999). What effective general managers really do. *Harvard Business Review, 77*(2), 145–156.

Krackhardt, D., & Hanson, J. R. (1993). Informal networks: The company behind the chart. *Harvard Business Review, 74*(4), 104–111.

Provan, K. G., Fish, A., & Sydow, J. (2007). Interorganizational networks at the network level: A review of the empirical literature on whole networks. *Journal of Management, 33,* 479–516.

Uzzi, B., Amaral, L., & Reed-Tsochas, F. (2007). Small-world networks and management science: A review. *European Management Review, 4,* 77–91.

Uzzi, B., & Dunlap, S. (2005). How to build your network. *Harvard Business Review, 83*(12), 53–60.

Textbooks That Incorporate Social Network Tools

Bauer, T., & Erdogan, B. (2009). *Organizational behavior.* New York: Flat World Knowledge.

Carpenter, M. A. (2010). *Managing effectively in tough times.* Upper Saddle River, NJ: Pearson/Prentice Hall.

Carpenter, M. A., Bauer, T., & Erdogan, B. (2009). *Principles of management: A behavioral approach.* New York: Flat World Knowledge.

Carpenter, M. A., & Sanders, W. G. (2009). *Strategic management: A dynamic perspective* (2nd ed.). Upper Saddle River, NJ: Pearson/Prentice Hall.

Thompson, L. (2008). *Making the team: A guide for managers* (3rd ed.). Upper Saddle River, NJ: Pearson/Prentice Hall.

Teaching Cases[1]

Keith Ferrazzi, Stanford University CaseSeries, No.9-OB4-4

This Keith Ferazzi case lets students analyze the social network setting of Keith Ferrazzi. Ferrazzi had certainly come a long way. The son of a steelworker and a cleaning lady, he attended an elite elementary school and then a top prep school in Pennsylvania, followed by undergraduate work at Yale and then Harvard Business School. He was wooed by top consulting firms and ended up on the partner track at Deloitte Consulting, where he built the company's marketing function. He left consulting to become the chief marketing officer of Starwood Hotels and Resorts, eventually leaving the company to become CEO of YaYa Media. In 1997, he was named by Crain's *Chicago Business* as a member of the "40 Under

40." In 1999, he was also named one of the "Power 10" by *Business Marketing*, and in 2002 was named among the most creative Americans in *Who's Really Who*. The World Economic Forum named him a "Global Leader of Tomorrow." In the summer of 2003, Ferrazzi was at a key crossroads in his life. He had sold YaYa Media to a company called American Vantage. He questioned the opportunities for growth within YaYa and was considering a transition from the company into a new role. Ferrazzi faced two questions: First, what should he do? Should he work for a large company in a senior management position, ultimately seeking to become the CEO? Should he seek out another CEO position at a smaller, entrepreneurial company? Should he do something entirely different, such as turn his skill at networking and his interest in teaching others how to build relationships into a business? Second, what other bases of influence besides networking and building social relationships should or could he develop? An optional 9-minute video is available as well.

Heidi Roizen, Harvard Business School, No.9-800-228

This Heidi Roizen case provides students with an example of an effective social network and facilitates discussion of network types, content, costs, and benefits. Heidi Roizen, a venture capitalist at SoftBank Venture Capital and a former entrepreneur, maintains an extensive personal and professional network. She leverages this network to benefit both herself and others. The case considers the steps she's taken to build and cultivate a network that is both broad and deep. Two optional videos are available as well.

Mixi, Harvard Business School, No.9-709-413

The Mixi case helps students understand when social networks add most value to exciting business models. Kasahara, the founder and CEO of Mixi, the most successful Japanese online social network, is deciding between two strategic options: (a) business to consumer (B2C) or (b) consumer to consumer (C2C), to leverage the power of the social network. In the B2C option, Mixi would become a portal for online shopping for both digital content and tangible goods and charge the business sellers a fee. In the C2C option, Mixi would facilitate exchanges between Mixi's members through online flea markets or auctions and charge the members for successful transactions. In choosing between the two options, he has to consider other upstart networks, particularly in the field of mobile social networking.

Walt Disney's Dennis Hightower: Taking Charge, No.395055; Transnational Manager, Harvard Business School, No.395056

The first case is set in 1987, where Dennis Hightower was recruited from outside for a newly created position as head of Disney Consumer Products European operations. Hightower has to win initial acceptance of entrenched country managers, integrate the company's diverse subsidiaries closer together, and revitalize European operations. The assignment? To develop an action plan that Dennis Hightower should follow over the next 3 months. This helps students explore the key strategic and organizational challenges facing Hightower, what pace of change is appropriate for the situation, and how he should try to build credibility and support within the organization. The second case describes the actions taken by Dennis Hightower as president of Disney Consumer Products in Europe and the Middle East from 1988 to 1994. Focuses on how he has established a regional office and knit local operations closer together, the benefits that the process has generated, and the tensions it has created within the organization. The case ends with Hightower contemplating whether he should be changing directions, given the emerging strategic and organizational challenges. The case series helps students to reflect on the following issues: (a) how to manage a new role with a social network–based strategy, (b) how to convert a federation of independent international operations into a transnational network, (c) how to decide between incremental and radical organizational change, (d) how to engineer organizational change, and (c) how to identify when a change process has gone far enough so as to stop it or even reverse direction. Videos are available with this case series as well.

Can a Shy Person Learn to Network?
Harvard Management Update, No. U9609C

This case study helps students see how shy people can learn to network. The case considers a senior vice president in a financial institution who fears that his job may fall victim to changing business trends. Although he realizes that networking could help, he resists it. One expert says that a study shows that 88% of us identify ourselves as shy. So, how does one push through it? The experts advise paying attention to the three overlapping networks of contacts—the task network on the job, the career network in professional organizations, and the social network of friends and acquaintances. And remember, the true form of networking is not about getting a job but about making—and maintaining—good human relationships that are held together by mutual interests.

The Best Advice I Ever Got, *Harvard Business Review*, No. F0712F

This article helps students see how others learn about networking. By watching a colleague assemble diverse, high-performing teams, the CEO of the Boston Consulting Group learned the art of nurturing individual strengths and steering team members away from tasks that would expose their weaknesses.

Social Network Applications in Business

Managing Networked Businesses: Course Overview for Educators, Harvard Business School, No. 5-807-104

This article provides an overview for educators of concepts covered in the Harvard MBA elective course Managing Networked Businesses (MNB). MNB focuses on management challenges in businesses that exhibit network effects. Such businesses comprise a large and growing share of the global economy and confront distinctive management challenges. Due to the unusual microeconomic attributes of networked businesses, designing optimal business models is difficult, and managers often must cope with "winner-take-all" (WTA) competitive dynamics. WTA outcomes have profound implications not only for strategy decisions but also for choices about capital structure, organizational design, and government relations.

Managing Networked Businesses: Course Overview
for Students, Harvard Business School, No. 9-806-103

This article on provides an overview for students of the Harvard MBA elective course Managing Networked Businesses (MNB). MNB focuses on management challenges in businesses that exhibit network effects. The first section of the article explains that such businesses comprise a large and growing share of the global economy and confront distinctive management challenges. Due to the unusual microeconomic attributes of networked businesses, designing optimal business models is difficult, and managers often must cope with WTA competitive dynamics. WTA outcomes have profound implications for strategy decisions, and choices about capital structure, organizational design, and government relations. For this reason, MNB employs a general management perspective. The second section of the article reviews a set of core concepts covered in MNB and provides definitions of networks, network effects, and platforms. The final section briefly describes the organization and contents of MNB's modules.

Winner-Take-All in Networked Markets,
Harvard Business School, No. 9-806-131

This article provides a framework for analyzing platform structure for students of the Harvard MBA elective Managing Networked Businesses, which focuses on management challenges in businesses with network effects. The article discusses platform structure in new networked markets, that is, whether a market that exhibits network effects will be served by a single platform or by rival platforms. It defines "platforms" and "platform structure," describes factors that influence the odds that a WTA outcome will prevail, and presents a framework for analyzing these factors in combination to predict platform structure.

Strategies for Two-Sided Markets,
Harvard Business Review, No. R0610F

This article on two-sided markets includes a one-page preview that quickly summarizes the key ideas and provides an overview of how the concepts work in practice along with suggestions for further reading. If you listed the blockbuster products and services that have redefined the global business landscape, you'd find that many of them tie together two distinct groups of users in a network. Case in point: The most important innovation in financial services since World War II is almost certainly the credit card, which links consumers and merchants. The list would also include newspapers, HMOs, and computer operating systems—all of which serve what economists call two-sided markets, or networks. Newspapers, for example, bring together subscribers and advertisers; HMOs link patients to a web of health care providers and vice versa; operating systems connect computer users and application developers. Two-sided networks differ from traditional value chains in a fundamental way. In the traditional system, value moves from left to right: To the left of the company is cost; to the right is revenue. In two-sided networks, cost and revenue are both to the left and to the right, because the "platform" has a distinct group of users on each side. The platform product or service incurs costs in serving both groups and can collect revenue from each, although one side is often subsidized. Because of what economists call "network effects," these platform products enjoy increasing returns to scale, which explains their extraordinary impact. Yet most firms still struggle to establish and sustain their platforms. Their failures are rooted in a common mistake: In creating strategies for two-sided networks, managers typically rely on assumptions and paradigms that apply to products without network effects. As a result, they make many decisions that are wholly inappropriate for the economics of their industries. In this article, the authors draw on recent theoretical work to guide executives negotiating the challenges of two-sided networks.

Platform-Mediated Networks: Definitions and
Core Concepts, Harvard Business School, #807049

This article provides students with a vocabulary and framework for analyzing platform-mediated networks. It's designed for an introductory module on network effects in strategy, marketing, technology management, information systems, or entrepreneurship courses. In a two-step process, the article defines platform-mediated networks and introduces concepts central to their study. First, the article defines networks and network effects; explains how network effects influence users' willingness to pay for network access; describes factors that determine the strength of network effects; discusses how a network's success may depend on users' expectations about its growth prospects; defines network externalities and their significance; presents a taxonomy of networks based on the number of distinct user groups—sides—that they encompass; and explains why network effects should be viewed as demand-related rather than supply-related scale economies. Second, the article defines platforms; describes different roles that firms play in platform creation and maintenance; discusses platform boundaries, for example, the distinction between platform providers and network users; and presents schemes for categorizing platforms based on their principal function, the structure of the networks they serve, and who controls them.

Managing Networked Businesses: Platform Evolution
Module, Harvard Business School, No. 808063

This article offers an overview of conceptual content and pedagogical guidance for instructors using a six-session module, Platform Evolution from Managing Networked Businesses (MNB), a case-based MBA elective course on platform-mediated networks. The module explores the competitive dynamics of platform evolution and the management challenges that it poses, with a focus on three strategies: envelopment, interoperability, and licensing. With envelopment, one platform provider enters another's market with a multiplatform bundle, potentially seizing platform leadership from its target. With interoperability, previously incompatible but well-established rivals relax restrictions on cross-platform transactions. With licensing, a firm that formerly served as the sole source of platform goods and services licenses additional providers to harness their innovation and marketing capabilities.

Google, Harvard Business School, No. 9-806-105

This case provides a basis for students to analyze the strategic significance of network effects in search-related advertising and for Google's prospects in the portal, e-commerce intermediary, and desktop operating system businesses. Also, the case allows students to explore whether pursuit of the latter opportunities is consistent with Google's mission and the company's unique culture and bottom-up processes for managing innovation. The case describes Google's history, business model, governance structure, corporate culture, and processes for managing innovation. It also reviews Google's recent strategic initiatives and the threats they pose to Yahoo!, Microsoft, and eBay. Asks what Google should do next. One option is to stay focused on the company's core competence—that is, developing superior search solutions and monetizing them through targeted advertising. Another option is to branch into new arenas; for example, build Google into a portal like Yahoo! or MSN; extend Google's role in e-commerce beyond search, to encompass a more active role as an intermediary (like eBay) facilitating transactions; or challenge Microsoft's hegemony over the PC by developing software to compete with Microsoft Office and Windows.

Business Networks, Stanford University, No. 9-OB6-2

This case enables students to assess the value proposition of the firm, alternatives to the network and the social system that underlies it, and the potential other uses of the system. In addition, students gain an understanding of the forces that underpin the performance improvement process for which the networkers subscribe to the network. The case describes a small consulting business, Business Networks, led by Les Cunningham. The firm's primary product was the establishment of groups or "networks" of similar businesses and the facilitation of each network's biannual meetings. Owners of individual firms, called networkers, met to tackle each other's business problems and share solutions. The networks were formed of like-sized contracting organizations that specialized in similar lines of business. The case provides a description of one biannual meeting and perspective from network members on the pros and cons of the process of performance improvement.

LinkedIn, Harvard Business School, No. 9-709-426

The case depicts the strategic dilemmas that confront a successful technology company in a fluid, fast-changing competitive field. In June 2008, the online professional networking service LinkedIn became a $1 billion company. But CEO Dan Nye understood that LinkedIn faced several strategic dilemmas. LinkedIn, founded in 2002, had become the world's leading professional networking service (PNS) by 2008, with more than 23 million members. Aiming to "dominate the business of business networking," in Nye's words, LinkedIn allowed individual members to post a profile on the LinkedIn site and then to use the site's tools to search for job opportunities; to recruit job candidates; to find suppliers, partners, and customers; and to seek out expert advice. The company was also expanding into corporate services that would enable companies to build and manage their own online networks. With revenue sources that included advertising, premium subscriptions, job posting services, and business solutions, LinkedIn was on track to bring in revenues in 2008 of up to $100 million. A new funding round in mid-2008 yielded a $1 billion valuation for the company. Three key dilemmas confronted LinkedIn, however. First, at a time when the "walled garden" model of online community building was under siege, it had to decide how far it should open its platform to users. Second, in light of competition from highly popular social network services such as Facebook and MySpace, LinkedIn had to decide whether to incorporate social networking into its value proposition. Third, in an increasingly global business environment, it had to weigh the option of merging with its leading international competitor, XING.com.

Cyworld: Creating and Capturing Value in a Social Network, Harvard Business School, No. 9-509-012

The Cyworld case helps students understand (a) how to create and capture value in a social network, (b) consumer behavior as well as segmentation and targeting in social networks, and (c) tangible and intangible value of customers in a networked society. In May 2008, the new CEO of Cyworld, a social network company in Korea, had to decide how to create and capture value from his rapidly growing user base. Cyworld was founded in 1999, and in 2003 it was acquired by SK Telecom, a leading mobile service provider in Korea. By 2007, Cyworld had 21 million users and $95 million revenue—$65 million from paid items (music, virtual gifts, etc.), $15 million from mobile networking, and $15 million from advertising. The new CEO had to decide which of these three revenue sources he should focus on in the future and how this choice would influence the target customers, the service offerings, and the required capabilities.

MySpace, Harvard Business School, No. 9-708-499

This case, focusing on MySpace, covers value propositions, portfolio management, strategic alliances, competitive advantage, browsers, Internet, Web-enabled application, Web sites, network hubs, and networks. The case, set in late 2007, examines what MySpace—the largest online social network—should do to respond to its agile competitor, Facebook. Since its inception, MySpace had experienced phenomenal growth, acquiring 20 million members in its first 20 months of operation and another 70 million a year later, to become the most visited Web site in the United States. Its growth stalled around mid-2007, just a few months after Facebook had released its programming platform that allowed outside programmers to build applications using its social network data. The wealth of new applications on Facebook allowed the company to increase its membership by more than 15% in one month. To remain competitive, MySpace had to release its own platform, and now it needs to decide whether to build its own proprietary application platform or join OpenSocial, a Google-sponsored open-source platform.

Notes

Introduction

1. See, for example, Carpenter and Westphal (2001), Carpenter and Wade (2002), and Carpenter and Stajkovic (2006).

2. This survey is conducted annually for over 20 years. This interpretation draws from Burt (1987), and later discussion by Baker (2000, pp. 28–29).

3. I consider the seminal works in this area to include Burt (1992) and Granovetter (1974). Baker (1994, 2000) provides excellent, action-oriented writing on the topic of social capital. Similarly, I consider Cross and Parker (2004) to be the authoritative guide to social networks. Kilduff and Tsai (2004) provide an excellent guide to the academic side of social networks. Finally, a comprehensive social psychological perspective on networks is found in Goleman (2006).

Chapter 1

1. See Cross and Parker (2004).

2. See Krackhardt (1987), Krackhardt (1990), and Casciaro (1998).

3. A useful introduction to other myths about managing social networks is provided in Cross, Nohria, and Parker (2002).

4. See chapters 1 through 6 of Carpenter and Sanders (2009) for examples of such sources of competitive advantage.

5. Putnam (2000).

6. See Kacperczyk, Sanchez-Burks, and Baker (2009).

7. See, in particular, Carpenter and Sanders (2009, chap. 3) on the internal firm sources of competitive advantage and the criteria where a resource provides competitive advantage when it is valuable, rare, difficult to imitate or substitute, and able to be exploited by the organization.

8. See Putnam (2000, p. 19).

9. Kilduff and Tsai (2004, p. 1).

Chapter 2

1. Gladwell (2000, p. 34).
2. Undergraduates reported average of 6 contacts (*SD* 3) and density of .60; MBAs reported an average of 9 contacts (*SD* 4) and density of .4; executive MBAs reported an average of 13 contacts (*SD* 5) and density of .51.
3. For a comprehensive review, see Kilduff and Tsai (2004).
4. See Katz (1982).
5. See Burt (2004) or Ibarra and Hunter (2007).
6. For the seminal study, see Granovetter (1974).
7. See Granovetter (1995).
8. See a complete review of the case for social intelligence in Goleman (2006).
9. This puts the person essentially in the role of being a broker and spanning a "structural hole." See Burt (1992).
10. See Carpenter and Wade (2002).

Chapter 3

1. The "great, great, great," mantra comes from Boothman (2008).
2. See, for example, Granovetter (1995) and Baker (2000).
3. See, for example, Baker (2000) and Goleman (2006).
4. See Goleman (2006) and Gallo (2007), for a work-related summary.
5. See Boothman (2008).
6. See Goleman (2006, chap. 2).

Chapter 4

1. Quoted in Chambers (2008).
2. See the IBM Technical Report by Ehrlich and Carboni (2005), for a nice introduction to SNA as a consulting tool.
3. See Cross, Nohria, and Parker (2002).
4. Can be found at http://www.thenetworkroundtable.org, accessed January 9, 2009.
5. See Cross, Borgatti, and Parker (2002).
6. See Cross, Borgatti, and Parker (2002, pp. 30–31).
7. See Cross, Borgatti, and Parker (2002, pp. 30–31).
8. See Cross, Borgatti, and Parker (2002, p. 33).
9. See Catmull (2008).
10. See Smith and Craig (2009).
11. See Heine (1995).

Chapter 5

1. See Fleming and Marx (2006). A great review of the small-world literature is found in Uzzi, Amaral, and Reed-Tsochas (2002).
2. "How Companies Approach Innovation" (2007).
3. Adapted from http://www.mckinseyquarterly.com, accessed June 4, 2008.
4. See Mindrum (2007).
5. See Friedman (2005).
6. Bartlett and Ghoshal (1997) introduced the notion of the "individualized corporation," where great companies are defined by purpose, process, and people. That notion is extended here to encompass current and future customers, as well as other key stakeholders.
7. See Quinn (1992, pp. 120–21).
8. See Friedman (2005, p. 194).
9. See Mindrum (2007, p. 9).
10. See Mindrum (2007, p. 9).
11. Hamel (2007).
12. See Chambers (2008).
13. Cited from Chambers (2008, p. 3).
14. Cited from Chambers (2008, p. 6).
15. Classmates Media S1 IPO Public Registration Filing, July 2007, U.S. Securities and Exchange Commission.
16. http://www.classmatesmedia.com/graphics/pdf/news/Classmates_Media_Corporation_Withdraws_IPO.pdf
17. http://blogs.zdnet.com/BTL/?p=7322, accessed November 4, 2008.

Chapter 6

1. I have adapted these ethical concerns from Borgatti and Molina (2003, 2005).
2. See Borgatti and Molina (2005).
3. To foster creativity, 3M encourages technical staff members to spend up to 15% of their time on projects of their own choosing. Also known as the "bootlegging" policy, the 15% rule has been the catalyst for some of 3M's most famous products, such as Scotch Tape and, of course, Post-it Notes. http://solutions.3m.com/wps/portal/3M/en_HK/post-it/index/post-it_past_present/history/the_whole_story?PC_7_RJH9U523086C5023CPSB8R18O2_assetType=MMM_Article&PC_7_RJH9U523086C5023CPSB8R18O2_assetId=1180595718358&PC_7_RJH9U523086C5023CPSB8R18O2_univid=1180595718358, accessed November 17, 2008.
4. See Borgatti and Molina (2005).
5. See Borgatti and Molina (2005, p. 110).

6. Adapted from Hartman and DesJardins (2008).
7. Adapted Borghatti and Molina (2005).
8. See Borghatti and Molina (2005, p. 112).
9. Baker (2000, pp. 23–24).

Appendix D

1. All the cases listed here are available through the Harvard Business School Publishing Web site at http://harvardbusinessonline.hbsp.harvard.edu.

References

Baker, W. E. (1994). *Networking smart*. New York: McGraw-Hill.

Baker, W. E. (2000). *Achieving success through social capital*. New York: Jossey-Bass.

Bartlett, C., & Ghoshal, S. (1997). *The individualized corporation: A fundamentally new approach to management*. New York: Harper Perennial Press.

Boothman, N. (2008). *How to make people like you in 90 seconds or less*. New York: Workman.

Borgatti, S. P., & Molina, J.-L. (2003). Ethical and strategic issues in organizational network analysis. *Journal of Applied Behavioral Science, 39*(3), 337–349.

Borghatti, S. P., & Molina, J.-L. (2005). Toward ethical guidelines for network research in organizations. *Social Networks, 27*, 107–117.

Burt, R. S. (1987). A note on the General Social Survey's ersatz network density item. *Social Networks, 9*, 75–85.

Burt, R. S. (1992). *Structural holes*. Boston: Harvard University Press.

Burt, R. S. (2004). Structural holes and good ideas. *American Journal of Sociology, 110*, 349–399.

Carpenter, M. A., & Sanders, W. G. (2009). *Strategic management: A dynamic perspective*. Upper Saddle River, NJ: Prentice Hall.

Carpenter, M. A., & Stajkovic, A. (2006). Social network theory and methods as tools for helping business confront global terrorism: Capturing the case and contingencies presented by dark social networks. In G. Suder (Ed.), *Corporate strategies under international terrorism and adversity* (pp. 7–19). New York: Edward Elgar.

Carpenter, M. A., & Wade, J. (2002). Micro-level opportunity structures as determinants of non-CEO executive pay. *Academy of Management Journal, 45*, 1085–1103.

Carpenter, M. A., & Westphal, J. D. (2001). The impact of director appointments on board involvement in strategic decision making. *Academy of Management Journal, 44*, 639–660.

Casciaro, T. (1998). Seeing things clearly: Social structure, personality and accuracy in social network perception. *Social Networks, 20*, 331–351.

Catmull, E. (2008). How Pixar fosters collective creativity. *Harvard Business Review, 86*(9), 64–73.

Chambers, J. (2008). Cisco sees the future: An interview with John Chambers. *Harvard Business Review, 86*(11), 1–8.

Cross, R., Borgatti, S., & Parker, A. (2002). Making invisible work visible. *California Management Review, 44*(2), 25–46.

Cross, R., Nohria, N., & Parker, A. (2002). Six myths about informal networks—and how to overcome them. *MIT Sloan Management Review, 43*(3), 67–75.

Cross, R., & Parker, A. (2004). *The power of social networks*. Boston: HBS Press.

Ehrlich, K., & Carboni, I. (2005). *IBM technical report: Inside social network analysis*. Armonk, NY: IBM.

Fleming, L., & Marx, M. (2006). Managing creativity in small worlds. *California Management Review, 48*(4), 6–27.

Friedman, T. (2005). *The world is flat: A brief history of the twenty-first century*. New York: Farrar, Straus, and Giroux.

Gallo, C. (2007, February 14). Body language: A key to success in the workplace. *Business Week*, pp. 23–24.

Gitomer, J. (2006) *Little black book of connections: 6.5 assets for networking your way to rich relationships*. Austin, TX: Bard Press.

Gladwell, M. (2000). *The tipping point: How little things can make a big difference*. New York: Little Brown & Company.

Goleman, D. (2006). *Social intelligence*. New York: Bantam.

Granovetter, M. (1974). *Getting a job: A study of contacts and careers*. Chicago: University of Chicago Press.

Granovetter, M. (1995). *Getting a job: A study of contacts and careers* (2nd ed.). Chicago: University of Chicago Press.

Hamel, G. (2007) *The future of management*. Boston: HBS Press.

Hartman, L., & DesJardins, J. (2008). *Business ethics: Decision-making for personal integrity and social responsibility*. New York: McGraw-Hill.

Heine, K. (1995, March). Sphinx paves the way to discover. *Focus*. NJ: Eli Lilly.

How companies approach innovation: A McKinsey global survey. (2007, October). *McKinsey QuarterlyOnline*.

Ibarra, H., & Hunter, M. (2007). How leaders create and use networks. *Harvard Business Review, 85*(1), 2–8.

Kacperczyk, A., Sanchez-Burks, J., & Baker, W. E. (2009). Social isolation in the workplace: A cross-cultural and longitudinal analysis. Unpublished working paper.

Katz, R. (1982). The effects of group longevity on project communication and performance. *Administrative Science Quarterly, 27*, 81–104.

Kilduff, M., & Tsai, W. (2004). *Social networks and organizations*. London: Sage.

Krackhardt, D. (1987). Cognitive social structures. *Social Networks, 9*, 109–134.

Krackhardt, D. (1990). Assessing the political landscape: Structure, cognition and power in organizations. *Administrative Science Quarterly, 35*, 342–369.

Mindrum, C. (2007). *Outsourcing learning and innovation in a flat world*. New Jersey: Accenture.

Post-it note history. Retrieved January 29, 2009, from http://solutions.3m.com/wps/portal/3M/en_HK/post-it/index/post-it_past_present/history/.

Putnam, R. (2000). *Bowling alone: The collapse and revival of American community*. New York: Simon & Schuster.

Quinn, J. B. (1992). *Intelligent enterprise: A knowledge and service based paradigm for industry*. New York: Free Press.

Scott, J. (2007). *Social network analysis*. London: Sage.

Smith, R., & Craig, S. (2009, January 6). Culture clash: Broker chief for Merrill quits BofA. *Wall Street Journal*, p. C1.

The Network Roundtable. Retrieved January 9, 2009, from http://www.thenetworkroundtable.org.

Uzzi, B., Amaral, L., & Reed-Tsochas, F. (2007). Small-world networks and management science: A review. *European Management Review, 4*, 77–91.

Index

Note: The italicized *f* and *t* following page numbers refer to figures and tables, respectively.

A

Accenture, 61–64
accessing social networks, 36–40
access networks, 81–82
adjusting social networks, 30–35
agendas of social networks, 42–43
aggressive networking, 36–37
assessment exercise, networks, 82–88
attitudes conducive to building social networks, 89–90
attributes, 77
authenticity of social networks, 30–31

B

Baker, Wayne, 75
Bank of America, 55
behaviors
   conducive to building social networks, 89–90
   useful for social networks, 24–29
beliefs, social networks and, 24–29
betweenness centrality, 7, 77
Boothman, Nicholas, 23, 43
Borgatti, Steve, 52, 71–72
boundary spanner, 7, 77
branding, 36–37
bridging ties, 19
business, social networks as, 66–67
Business Networks, 100
Business Press Publications, 91–93

C

careers, networks and, 18–19, 18*f*, 81–82
cases. teaching, 93–102
cataloging members of social networks, 35
centrality, 7, 77
Chambers, John, 49, 65
Cisco Systems, 49, 64–65
Classmates Media, 66–67
clique, 7, 77
collaboration, 40, 49–56, 63–64
communication networks, 81–82
comparing
   network size and density among students, 13*t*
   vertical and horizontal organizations, 62*f*
Connect + Develop product development strategy, 57–58
connectors, 77
consistency of social networks, 30–31
contacts, network, 83
critical persons, 7
Cross, Rob, 50, 52–54, 58
Cyworld, 101–2

D

data collection for social network analysis (SNA), 51
Dawes, William, 8–9

density, 77, 84
    comparing among students, 13*t*
    networks, 84
direction of relationship, 78
distance, 78
diverse opinions, social networks and, 26–27
dyad, 78

E

egocentric networks, 78
ethical issues, 69–75
    informed consent, 73
    privacy, 69–70
exchange networks, 15
exchange principle, 14, 16–17, 20

F

Facebook, 3, 5, 66, 101–2
feeding social networks, 36–40
Ferrazzi, Keith, 93–94
focal groups, in social network analysis, 50–51

G

General Social Survey (GSS), 1–2
Goleman, Daniel, 41
Google, 65, 99–102
Granovetter, Mark, 18–19, 45
grids, network, 84–88

H

Hamel, Gary, 64–65
Hightower, Dennis, 95
horizontal organizations, 61–65, 62*f*–63*f*

I

individual performance, social networks and, 11–21
informal networks, 3–4, 40

information networks, 81–82
informed consent, 73
initiatives, social networks, 40–44
innovation networks, 57–59
    activities underlying each phase of, 60*t*
    management, 59*f*
isolate, 78

J

judging in social networks, 41–42

K

knowledge networks, 81

L

Lilly, Eli, 55–56
LinkedIn, 3, 5, 66, 101
listening skills, 46

M

maintaining relationships, 27–28
managing social networks, 30–35
McCann, Bob, 55
McKinsey & Company, 57–61
members, network, 78
Merrill Lynch, 55
Milgram, Stanley, 11–12, 16
Mixi, 94–95
Molina, Jose-Luis, 71–72
multipurpose networks, 33–34
MySpace, 66, 101–2
myths about social networks, 3–4

N

networked organizations, 17, 20–21, 61
networks. *See* social networks
nodes, network, 78
Nohria, Nitin, 50

INDEX   113

O

opportunities, social networks, 25–26
organizations
    networked, 17, 20–21, 61
    vertical and horizontal, 61–65, 62f–63f
outlier, 78
overload, social networks, 31–32

P

Parker, Andrew, 50, 52
Pixar, 20, 55
Platform Evolution, 99
platform-mediated networks, 98–99
principle of exchange, 14, 16–17, 20
principle of reciprocity, 14, 38
principle of similarity, 14
privacy, 69–70
problem-solving networks, 81–82
Procter & Gamble (P&G), 57–58
Putnam, Robert, 4, 6

R

reachability, 78
readings
    business press publications, 91–93
    social network analysis methods, 91
    social network textbooks, 93
reciprocity principle, 14, 38
relationships
    direction of, 78
    type of, 79
Revere, Paul, 8–9
Roizen, Heidi, 94

S

scheduling social networks, 34–35
self-assessment survey, 81–88
separation, six degrees of, 11
shyness, networking and, 45–48, 96

similarity principle, 14
six degrees of separation, 11
size of social networks, 15–16, 78
small-world social networks, 11–12
SNA. *See* social network analysis (SNA)
social capital, 5–6, 79
social network analysis (SNA), 6, 50–56, 69, 72–74
    data collection, 51
    focal groups, 50–51
    readings, 91
    survey design, 51
    targeted, 52–56
social networks, 5–6, 78, 79
    access, 36–40, 81–82
    adjusting, 30–35
    agendas, 42–43
    aggressive networking, 36–37
    attitudes, 89–90
    authenticity, 30–31
    behaviors, 24–29, 89–90
    beliefs, 24–29
    branding, 37
    as business, 66–67
    careers and, 18–19, 18f, 81–82
    cataloging members, 35
    changes to fit job, 32–33
    communication, 81–82
    consistency, 30–31
    contacts, 83
    creating, 23–48
    density, 13t, 77, 84
    diagram, 7f
    diverse opinions, 26–27
    egocentric, 78
    exchange, 15
    feeding, 36–40
    grid, 86–87
    horizontal organizations, 63f
    individual performance and, 11–21
    informal, 3–4, 40
    information, 81–82
    initiatives, 40–44
    innovation, 59t–60t
    judging by looks, 41–42

social networks (*continued*)
  knowledge, 81
  listening skills, 46
  maintaining relationships, 27–28
  managing, 30–35
  members, 78
  multipurpose, 33–34
  myths about, 3–4
  nodes, 78
  opportunities, 25–26
  overload, 31–32
  problem-solving, 81–82
  reciprocity principle, 14, 38
  scheduling, 34–35
  self-assessment, 81–88
  shyness and, 45–48, 96
  size, 13t, 15–16, 78
  small-world, 11–12
  survey participant disclosure, 73f
  target, 79
  ties, 6, 18–19, 18f, 39–40, 78
  values, 24–29
  as work, 28–29
Sphinx Pharmaceuticals, 55–56
strength of relationship, 79
strong ties, 18–19
students, comparing among, 13t

surveys
  design, 51
  participant disclosure, 73f
  self-assessment, 81–88

T

targeted social network analysis (SNA), 52–56
target network, 79
teaching cases, 93–102
Telepresence, 65
ties, 6, 78
  bridging, 19
  strong, 18–19
  weak, 18–19, 18f, 39–40

V

values, social networks and, 24–29
vertical organizations, 62f

W

Walt Disney Company, 55, 95
weak ties, 18–19, 18f, 39–40